DO Y

* How your hand can m   y
across the printed page?

* How increasing your "span of perception" will make you
read faster?

* Why you need to use different techniques for reading a magazine article and for a nonfiction book?

* How often you should look away from a computer screen to
maximize speed and comprehension?

* Why reading in both directions is twice as fast as reading in
only one?

* Why technical material may be easier to read than other
printed matter—but comprehension may fall by 50% unless
you know the secrets of reading it?

* Why natural light may be the wrong illumination for computer use?

* How to beat one of the most common reading problems . . .
in just 15 minutes?

**GET THE ANSWERS
AND GET RESULTS WITH . . .**
21st CENTURY GUIDE TO INCREASING YOUR READING SPEED

21ST CENTURY GUIDE TO INCREASING YOUR READING SPEED

- **TAKE IN ONE MILLION WORDS OR MORE PER WEEK!**
- **TRIPLE YOUR READING SPEED FOR BUSINESS LETTERS**
- **IMPROVE YOUR STUDY SKILLS AND READING COMPREHENSION**
- **SAVE TIME AND REDUCE EYESTRAIN WHEN READING FROM COMPUTER SCREENS**

EDITED BY THE PRINCETON LANGUAGE INSTITUTE

LAURIE E. ROZAKIS, PH. D., COMPILER
ELLEN LICHTENSTEIN, SPECIAL CONSULTANT

L A U R E L

A LAUREL BOOK

Published by
Dell Publishing
a division of Bantam Doubleday Dell Publishing Group, Inc.
1540 Broadway
New York, NY 10036

Published by arrangement with The Philip Lief Group, Inc.
6 West 20th Street
New York, New York 10011

ISBN: 0-440-21724-5

Printed in the United States of America

Published simultaneously in Canada

March 1995

10   9   8   7   6   5   4   3

Contents

4. Words, Words, Words: Using Speed-Reading Techniques Within Text

5. The Super Six: Reading Methods for the Information Age

6. Not All Reading Is the Same!

7. Common Reading Problems and How to Solve Them

8. Self Tests

Index

Introduction

> After more than a century of electric technology, we have
> extended our central nervous system itself into a global
> embrace, abolishing both space and time as far as our planet is
> concerned.

As of 1995, about twenty-five years have passed since a then-
unknown scholar at the University of Toronto penned this
warning. In a document called *Understanding Media*, Marshall
McLuhan prophesied the worldwide coming together of human
awareness into a single community. He called this unification
the "global village." Who today would argue with McLuhan's
vision? In 1992, the world watched the citizens of Eastern
Europe toss out decades of history. A sprawling computer network joins users in 35 countries. Trading on the Tokyo stock
market can give a New York broker indigestion at breakfast.

The 21st Century: Frontiers of
Vast Technological Change

These changes are only the beginning of what the 21st century
holds in store for us. The developing world is undergoing a
remarkable convergence of computing and communications
technology, the impact of which, according to experts, will
rival that of the Industrial Revolution. This transformation of

global life is already apparent in a glittering roll call of technological advancements, such as fax machines, automatic teller machines, streamlined laptop and portfolio computers, VCRs, telephone answering machines, modems, floppy disks, hypertext, virtual reality, videotext, call waiting, compact disks, CD-ROMs, cellular phones, video games, interactive toys, and high-definition TVs.

Industrial and academic laboratories are creating technologies that will make today's innovations tomorrow's dinosaurs, lumbering and clumsy creatures useful only as children's amusements. Technological globalization will upend skill needs, turn the very notion of a career on its head, and drastically restructure whole sections and regions of the economy. It is all right around the corner. Blink and it will be here.

A Deluge of Information

The chances are excellent that you have already been bombarded with more information than you can possibly read, much less absorb. How can you keep up with the dizzying rate of social, political, geographic, and economic change around the world?

With the technological explosion, reading experts believe that the average worker in a position of average responsibility is expected to read up to *one million* words in a single week! A typical businessperson is required to read

- Five or six books a month
- Technical and professional journals
- Three to five general magazines a week
- Fifty letters a day.

According to current estimates, more than 12,000 medical journals are published every year. That means that a physician could read a page a minute for eight hours every day and still not cover all the material published every year in the medical field!

Think about the piles of printed material you have to plow through every week at the office: business letters, interoffice memos, year-end reports, trade journals, assessment forms, technical articles, newspapers, order forms, rush faxes, invoices, and evaluation forms. You may have to read text-books, school forms, community newspapers, magazines, and club information as well. And there are all those novels, short stories, plays, magazines, and newspapers that you would like to read but that stay piled up beside the recliner. The list can go on and on, as the flood of information threatens to drown us in print and electronic media.

How to Cope with the Information Explosion

At first glance, the problem may seem insoluble. It's not. You *can* learn to read faster and retain more. This book will teach you simple, proven ways to read for information and to retain what you read. You will learn time-tested techniques such as skimming, backward reading, space reading, key words, pre reading, and critical reading. What do you need? Just the desire and willingness to improve your reading. By using this book, you will be able to

- Increase your reading speed
- Reach your best reading speed
- Enlarge your reading comprehension
- Remember important information more easily
- Concentrate on your work more effectively
- Improve your study skills.

But today's frantic lifestyle leaves little room for reading and studying. One of the best things about improving your reading speed and comprehension is that it requires a minimum commitment of study time — and this initial commitment will pay off a thousandfold. If you spend just a few minutes every day with this book, we can help you master your reading load. How much time? Set aside 15 minutes a day — that's all. Use the time on the bus or the train when you commute to work. How about the time you spend standing in lines, sitting in a doctor's office, or waiting in the car? This small investment of time will help you master skills that will last a lifetime.

All it takes is practice. Within a few weeks you should see remarkable progress, not only with your professional or technical reading, but with everything you read. And you'll feel your reading load shrink!

How well you read can affect both the success of your company and your career. Reading well can also expand your personal life. For the better you read, the more enjoyment you will get from reading. You can join local literary or library study groups and share ideas with others. You can broaden personal interests with more advanced reading. Make the time you spend on this book productive — but also make it enjoyable. Relax and get ready to see remarkable improvement in your reading skills.

> Triple your reading rate and you will save yourself two or more hours a day. This can save your company thousands of dollars a year! And the rewards to you will be incalculable.

Twenty-five Reasons to Become a Better Reader

1. To increase my knowledge
2. To increase my reading enjoyment
3. To better understand what I'm reading
4. To get information that I need on the job
5. To be a more valuable employee
6. To help me get ahead in my career
7. To be a more effective team player
8. To be able to ask insightful questions
9. To earn a promotion and/or a raise

10. To get facts that I need in my personal life
11. To make more accurate evaluations of situations
12. To help prevent errors and misjudgments
13. To help others improve their education
14. To increase my vocabulary skills
15. To become a better speaker and communicator
16. To understand political issues and views different from mine
17. To gather needed background information
18. To compare ideas more effectively
19. To improve my writing skills
20. To be a more efficient and disciplined worker
21. To make better decisions
22. To feel better about myself
23. To foster my creativity
24. To understand the latest innovations in my field
25. To increase my job satisfaction

What reasons of your own can you add? Why is it important to you to be a better reader?

1

Getting Started

Speed-reading is useless if you do not understand what you are reading. Accurate comprehension will be one of your reading goals. Here are a few sample passages to help you see how your reading comprehension stacks up. Read through the passages that follow and answer the questions. Read at your normal rate—don't rush and try to save time. Remember, this test is for you! Then check the answer key at the end to see your score.

Passage A: Space, the Final Frontier

Do you want to look into the future? Just cast an eye skyward. One hundred miles overhead—at a distance only half as far as that between Boston and New York—is an environment of extraordinary characteristics. You are gazing at a new realm of resources.

In today's world of increasing global competition, space represents an economic frontier, a new territory of commercial opportunity. Scientific discovery and technological innovations can benefit people throughout the world, resulting in entirely new industries. Space is proving to be a fertile field for such economic growth.

Space commerce is composed of diverse activities that fall into four broad areas: satellite communications, Earth and ocean observations, materials research and processing, and space transportation and industrial services.

Satellite communications, while well established and mature, continues to develop through new applications and advanced technology. Yet this 3-billion-dollar-a-year industry did not even exist 25 years ago!

Observing our planet from space has already produced immense public benefit through improved weather forecasting and monitoring of resources and the environment. Valuable commercial applications of regular Earth observations are becoming increasingly practical through advances in computer processing and interpretations of remote sensing data from specially equipped satellites.

Space has become an industrial laboratory for materials research processing. Today's research and development work, being carried out under government and corporate sponsorship, is expected to lead to new scientific and technological breakthroughs.

There is tantalizing evidence that unique products of high value may be processed in the weightless high vacuum of space. It is also possible that what industrial researchers learn in space could dramatically change the way materials are processed in factories on Earth. Many people believe this area offers the greatest potential for economic benefit. The possibilities are virtually limitless.

These commercial uses of space, coupled with the requirements of government space programs, are prompting the emergence of a commercial space transportation industry. With broad, worldwide demand for access to space, this is the most competitive of the current commercial space activities. Various other industrial support services are also being offered commercially.

Business in space is not business as usual. The expansion of space commerce faces substantial challenges associated with cost, risk, and competition on Earth. But private enterprise is adapting to the environment of space, attracted by the potential returns from tapping new resources.

Questions

Read each of the following questions and circle the best answer. Write down how much time it takes you to answer these questions in the space provided.

1. How far is space above earth?
   a. 100 miles   c. 200 miles
   b. 300 miles   d. 400 miles

2. What does space represent to the author?
   a. a realm of great fear yet great potential
   b. an untapped region that promises more than it can deliver
   c. an economic frontier
   d. a place where Earth people can one day go to live

3. How many areas are there in space commerce?
   a. 1   b. 2   c. 3   d. 4

4. Which of the following choices is *not* one of these areas?
   a. materials research and processing
   b. space teleportation

c. satellite communications

d. Earth and ocean observations

5. How much income does satellite communications generate every year?
   a. 1 million dollars
   b. 3 million dollars
   c. 3 billion dollars
   d. 30 billion dollars

6. What two public benefits has space already produced?
   a. improved weather forecasting and discovery of new minerals
   b. better environmental control and mineral processing
   c. environmental waste reduction and mineral discoveries
   d. improved weather forecasting and monitoring of the environment and resources

7. What is today's research and development work expected to lead to?
   a. new scientific and technological breakthroughs
   b. reduced profits
   c. new ways to control people
   d. increased spending on a national level

8. What area is expected to offer the greatest economic benefit?
   a. weather forecasting
   b. computer processing
   c. materials research processing
   d. reduction of environmental hazards

9. Which is the most competitive area of commercial space activities?
   a. recycling environmental waste
   b. the commercial space transportation industry
   c. materials processing
   d. space travel

10. How is business in space funded?
    a. public funds only   c. private funds only
    b. public and private funds d. academic grants

Total time: _____

Answers

1. a   2. c   3. d   4. b   5. c
6. d   7. a   8. c   9. b   10. b

How well do you comprehend what you read?

Superior readers   answered all questions right in 5 minutes
Good readers   answered all questions right in 10 minutes
Poor readers   answered all questions right in 15 minutes

Passage B: On Borrowed Time?

The 21st century has already come to many workers—with good and bad results. Read on to see how these drastic changes in the work force might affect *you!*

What happens when a company loses a chief operating officer? The traditional approach was to fill the position as quickly as possible, either by promoting a proven worker from within the ranks or by hiring a new manager from outside. Often, this was done very quickly.

In recent years, however, businesses have been toying with a vastly different solution: retaining an experienced executive on a temporary basis. Companies benefit in a number of ways. First, they have an experienced leader at the helm. As a result, they can take their time looking for a permanent replacement. In addition, there is a significant savings to the bottom line, since the temporary replacement rarely receives the benefits of a full-time worker. With compensation packages at one-third of salary base in many firms, this represents very real savings.

The use of temporary executives is just one example of a disturbing new trend in businesses around the world. In the United States, Japan, the United Kingdom, France, Germany, and other countries, employers are turning to temporary workers for a wide range of functions. In 1992 alone, temporary employee placements in U.S. firms soared to nearly as many workers as were hired for new full-time jobs in the private sector. From blue-collar factory workers to highly trained specialists in a number of fields, temporary employees are helping businesses stay competitive. Many firms, especially those needing help at peak seasons, find it more economical to hire temps than to add permanent staff requiring health care and other costly benefits.

Without a doubt, temporary employment is not a new practice. For centuries, agricultural workers have held temporary jobs, with work restricted to harvesttime or other peak periods. Within the past 100 years, the industrial sector has depended at various times on temporary workers. During World War II, for example, large numbers of women took factory jobs to replace men who were serving in the military. More recently, the temporary use of secretaries and other clerical workers has become commonplace.

What is new is the scope of temporary services in the contemporary workplace. Today's "temp" may be a computer programmer, attorney, engineer, or accountant. Writers, sales managers, drafters, pharmacists, artists, physicians, lawyers, and various levels of managers are just a few of the many types of workers whose jobs have been filled by "temps." In fact, according to the U.S. Department of Labor, during an average day, more than a million people are employed through some form of temporary service in the United States. Between 5 and 8 percent of all employees in

England and Germany hold temporary positions. Even Japan, with its traditional emphasis on long-term job stability, has experienced a growing dependence on temporary and part-time workers.

Critics of temporary employment point out that such employees become something of an underclass, because the employer does not owe them any type of permanent job rights. They may not get health benefits or pensions, for example, and their employment can be terminated at the employer's pleasure, without advance notice or legal recourse. It would be a mistake, however, to assume that all temporary workers would prefer permanent jobs. On the contrary, many temporary workers find that the arrangement allows them to combine their personal and business lives in a much more advantageous way.

Some are retired people who want to keep active in their fields, but only on a limited basis. Others are students and teachers. Still others are parents who see temporary work as an ideal compromise between working full-time and spending more time with their families. Some people simply prefer the freedom that comes with temporary employment. They are free to pursue personal interests between work assignments, including traveling, studying, hobbies, or just avoiding job stress.

Questions

Read each of the following questions and circle the best answer. Write down how much time it takes for you to answer these questions in the space provided.

1. Hiring a temporary worker has all the following advantages to the employer except:
   a. gaining flexibility
   b. hiring an experienced person
   c. sacrificing money
   d. saving on benefit packages

2. Overall, the trend has been to hire _____ temporary workers as full-time employees.
   a. fewer   c. as many
   b. more   d. a decreasing number of

3. Hiring temporary workers is a(n) _____ idea.
   a. relatively new   c. 20th century
   b. 21st century   d. old

4. During World War II, _____ became temporary
   workers.
   a. children   c. women
   b. men   d. immigrants

5. How many people are employed as temporary workers on
   an average day in the United States?
   a. 1 million   c. 2 million
   b. 3 million   d. 4 million

6. What percentage of the work force in the United Kingdom
   is temporary labor?
   a. 1–2 percent   c. 2–4 percent
   b. 4–5 percent   d. 5–8 percent

7. People who oppose the trend toward temporary labor
   argue that it
   a. discriminates against employers
   b. is unfair to employees
   c. shuts out qualified managers
   d. is a mistake, because all workers want permanent jobs

8. Employees who favor temp work believe that it
   a. pays better than full-time work
   b. does not allow them free time to pursue other interests

c. discriminates against the elderly

d. can afford them much greater freedom than full-time work

Total time: _____

Answers

1. c   2. b   3. d   4. c

5. a   6. d   7. b   8. d

How well do you comprehend what you read?

Superior readers   answered all questions right in 10 minutes

Good readers   answered all questions right in 15 minutes

Poor readers   answered all questions right in 20 minutes

LESSON TWO: MEASURING YOUR INITIAL READING SPEED

Before you can begin to pick up reading speed, you have to measure your initial reading rate. As your reading speed increases, you can refer back to this section to gauge your progress.

Use the following passage to determine your current reading rate. Here's how to do it:

1. Get an alarm that you can set for one minute. An alarm clock, egg timer, or watch with an alarm will work well. Set it to ring one minute after you begin reading.

2. When the alarm rings, stop reading. Determine the line number you stopped at.

3. Multiply the number of lines read by 10 (the average

number of words per line including the title). This will give you your initial reading speed.

Sample Passage

If after one minute you have read through line 30 of the following text, multiply 30 by 10. Your initial reading speed is 300 words per minute.

Satellite Communications

Satellite communications was the first, and is today the most mature, of the commercial uses of space. In just 25 years, this technology has produced an industry that generates $3 billion in annual revenues, has created entirely new fields of employment, and has transformed the very way that business is conducted on Earth.

On July 10, 1962—five months after John Glenn became the first American to orbit Earth—a 170-pound satellite called
10 *Telstar* was rocketed into space atop a NASA Delta booster.

While much of the nation's attention toward space was riveted on the unfolding race for landing humans on the moon, *Telstar* 1, the world's first satellite built and paid for by private industry, launched a revolution in tele-communications that marked the beginnings of space commerce. *Telstar* was designed and developed at Bell Telephone Labs to show that an orbiting spacecraft could actively relay signals from one point on Earth to another. Within hours following the launch, Bell engineers had
20 successfully relayed telephone and TV transmissions, and soon afterward, the first "via satellite" TV programming was relayed across the Atlantic.

A year later, the NASA-developed *Syncom* satellite pioneered research into the use of communications satellites

positioned at a distance where their orbital period is
synchronized with Earth's rotation, and the spacecraft
therefore remains in the same position over Earth. The
territory of space has become increasingly congested as
nation after nation has joined the space age by orbiting its
30 own communications spacecraft and international systems.

Communications satellites now carry more than two-
thirds of the world's international voice communications, and
transmit nearly all of the world's video programming.
Demand by communication satellite owners and operators
for access to space remains strong, accounting for virtually
all of the present-day private-sector market for commercial
launch services.

Worldwide, communications satellite billings by U.S. and
foreign manufacturers totaled about $1 billion in 1987, with
40 sales by American manufacturers accounting for about half
the total. Projected total revenue from the sale and lease of
satellite transponders in 1987 was estimated at $1 billion.
Revenues to U.S. companies alone for domestic sales of
ground receiving equipment totaled about $7 billion in 1987.

A competitive challenge to satellite communications is
being posed by increasing use of fiber-optics cables. This
terrestrial technology challenge underscores one of the
continuing risks of space commerce.

Yet new markets for communications via satellite
50 continue to unfold. Radio determination satellite services,
which among other applications will allow a central control
center to track and monitor the location and status of trucks,
trains, aircrafts, and vessels, could become a major profit
center for the satellite industry. One firm already servicing
this new market, Geostar Corporation, will launch satellites
aboard NASA's space shuttle under a space systems
development agreement—which allows a deferred payback
of standard launch services costs.

Research and development work to advance satellite
60 communications is continuing in the U.S. and abroad. NASA,
for example, is working to develop advanced
communications technology. A key issue of this relatively
mature industry is how to properly continue to advance
technology. NASA's Office of Commercial Programs is
considering the possible establishment of a Center for
Commercial Development of Space, funded through
contributions by both government and industry, focused in
this area.

Earth and Ocean Observations

70 Commercial Earth and ocean observation from space is an
emerging area of space commerce that is being assisted by
privatization policies and the growth of a "value added"
industry based on the interpretation and analysis of satellite-
gathered data. Remote sensing observations, based on
space-based or airborne measurements of reflected or
emitted radiation, can reveal features and characteristics of
Earth's land and ocean surface that are difficult or
impossible to detect in ordinary photographs.

Advanced optical instruments and radar sensors collect
80 data in digital form, then send it back to Earth receiving
stations. Computer processing and enhancement of the
images can make the invisible visible. Since the beginning of
the space age, people have realized that the unique vantage
point of Earth orbit provides an unparalleled perspective of
our planet. The earliest application of this resource was the
use of meteorological satellites to provide a global picture of
weather patterns, resulting in vastly improved weather
forecasts.

In 1962, NASA launched the first Earth resources
90 technology satellite to demonstrate the usefulness of remote

sensing on a global and repetitive basis. Specifically, the mission of this satellite was to determine what data could be gathered by an automated spacecraft, how these data could be interpreted and applied to a broad range of endeavors, and how the information yield could be of economic or social value to commercial, scientific, and government interests. The spacecraft subsequently was renamed *Landstat* 1 and became the first of five *Landstat* spacecrafts orbited to date. The system was declared operational in 1973 and
100 transferred to the National Oceanic and Atmospheric Administration as part of a privatization program.

NASA's research and development programs demonstrated that remote observations from space can assist a wide diversity of Earth-based activities, such as exploring for oil, forecasting crop yields, managing forest resources, monitoring the environment, and documenting land uses. Today, the system is operated by the Earth Observation Satellite Corporation.

Reading Rate: _____

What's your reading rate? The average rate for untrained readers is between 150 and 400 words per minute with the comprehension rate about 70 percent. This is about a sixth-grade reading rate.

If you are reading below 100 words per minute, you might want to go through this book more than once. The extra reading will help you pick up things you may have missed the first time around.

Good readers have different reading rates for different reading tasks. Trained speed-readers might read newspaper articles at 1,500 words per minute, financial news at 1,000 words per minute, and novels at 800 words per minute. Technical materials often take the longest time of all, usually around 400–500 words per minute. Remember: speed is not the only consideration—you must understand what you read. Reading without comprehending is of no value.

If you are like most people, you are reading at about 20 to 25 percent of your maximum capacity. That leaves about 70 percent untapped! This book will help you tap your full potential.

Reading Rate

Average trained speed-reader	500–1,500 words per minute
Average untrained reader	150–400 words per minute
Average speaker	160 words per minute
Trained storyteller	140 words per minute

Speed-reading training can help you even if English is not your native language. However, you may want to adapt the techniques in this book to your native language *first*. If your English is very weak, read through the techniques in this book, and then try them out on a text written in your own language. Then come back to this book and read through the English passages. Once you have mastered the basic skills you need for speed-reading, you can apply them to any language.

LESSON THREE: MORE ON YOUR READING RATE

If you want to measure your reading rate on material outside this book, it's easy to do. Just remember that your rate will vary with the difficulty of the material. Follow this procedure:

1. Allow yourself one minute. Set the alarm clock, watch, or egg timer that you used before.
2. Read the passage.
3. Count the number of words in ten typical lines, not *sentences*. Total these numbers and divide by 10, to get the average number of words per line. Write down this number.

4. Count the number of lines you read. Multiply the number of lines by the average number of words per line. This will tell you how many words you can read in a minute.

Here's one more practice passage before we begin Lesson 4:

The Global Village: They Saw It Coming

In 1851, short story writer and novelist Nathaniel Hawthorne wrote in *The House of the Seven Gables:* "It is a fact . . . that, by means of electricity, the world of matter has become a great nerve, vibrating thousands of miles in a breathless point of time! Rather, the round globe is a vast head, a brain, instinct with intelligence! Or, shall we say, it is itself a thought, nothing but thought, and no longer the substance which we deemed it!"

10   In 1925, British writer Aldous Huxley wrote in *Those Barren Leaves:* "It is comforting to think, that modern civilization is doing its best to reestablish this tribal regime, but on an enormous national and even international scale. Cheap printing, wireless telephones, trains, motor cars, gramophones, and all the rest are making it possible to consolidate tribes, not of a few thousands, but of millions. In a few generations it may be that the whole planet will be covered by one vast American-speaking tribe, composed of innumerable individuals all thinking and acting in exactly the same way, like the characters 20 in a novel by Sinclair Lewis . . . .

"Mr. Cardan nodded and puffed at his cigar. 'That's certainly a possibility,' he said. 'A probability almost; for I don't see that it's in the least likely that we shall be able to breed a race of beings, at any rate within the next thousand years, sufficiently intelligent to be able to form a stable non-tribal society. Perhaps a slightly lower standard would be necessary.'"

Reading time: _____

Quick Hints for Faster Reading

1. Concentrate. Soft, regular background noise is better than absolute silence. Noninstrusive instrumental music is recommended.

2. Don't read if you are exhausted.

3. Don't read if something is distracting. You will be unable to concentrate and will find that your comprehension is way down.

4. Have your eyes checked regularly. Wear glasses or contact lenses if you need them.

5. Do not buy over-the-counter reading glasses. Always have your eyeglasses fitted by an optometrist or ophthalmologist.

6. Do not read for more than two hours without a break.

7. Read in natural light or under good artificial light. At the very least, there should be at least one 100-watt bulb with another light in the room to avoid glare.

8. Hold the reading material at a comfortable distance from your eyes, about 14 inches.

9. Position the book so the print at the top of the page will be the same distance from your eyes as the print at the bottom of the page.

10. Read in a hard chair at a desk. Don't read sprawled in a chair.

LESSON FOUR: WHAT IS SPEED READING FOR THE 21ST CENTURY?

To master the skills of speed reading, you need the following:

1. *A broad background of general information or a broad background in the area in which you will be doing most of your reading.*

   When you have a basic knowledge of the material you

are reading, you will be able to apply more *prior knowledge* to the text. You will not have to waste time figuring out the basic principles of the writer's thesis. This will enable you to grasp the writer's point more quickly, which will, in turn, greatly increase your reading speed.

2. *The vocabulary of the material that you will be reading.*
   Your reading will go much more quickly and smoothly when you and the writer are "speaking the same language." For example, if you are reading a piece on computers, your reading will be easier if you know such terms as "boot up," "ROM," and "hard copy." If you have to stop to figure out the basic vocabulary of the reading or look up the words in the dictionary, you will be reading at less than your optimal speed.

3. *A desire to improve.*
   While 21st century speed reading is not overly difficult to master, it does require effort on your part. You will make progress most quickly when you push yourself and want to learn. Go through the book carefully and complete all the exercises. Don't shortchange yourself!

4. *A positive attitude*
   You *can* do it! You will find your reading speed improving much more dramatically when you approach the task with an open mind and a positive attitude.

2

Using Hand Motions to Increase Reading Speed

The Importance of Hand Coordination

When you were a child, you learned to read individual letters and sounds. If you saw the word "cat," for example, you would say each letter, "c-a-t." Then you would form the sounds and finally decode the word. Now, of course, you read entire words, not individual letters. Most of the time, you're not even aware of the individual letters.

In many ways, speed-reading is like a great friendship: all the different elements seem to fall into place. One of the most important aspects of this relationship is the link between your eyes and the printed page. This blend of the mental and the mechanical is essential to superior reading speed and comprehension.

One of the best ways to improve your reading speed and comprehension is to train your hands and eyes to work as partners. Your hand coordinates your eye movements. Training your hands and eyes to work together on a text is one of the first steps to increasing reading speed. Our eyes tend to be lazy and jerky. They will move much more smoothly and quickly if we guide them with a finger on the page. Although there are different ways to coordinate eyes and hands, each method has the same purpose: to increase speed and comprehension.

In addition to turning pages, your hands can lead your eyes down the page with smooth, rapid motions. Like a good manager, the hand becomes the pacesetter, moving at a steady rate. How is this done?

- Your hand forces your eyes to move across the page. This can prevent you from overlooking important words.
- Your hand forces your eyes to move on to new lines of text. This helps prevent you from going back over and over the same lines — especially if you understood them the first time.
- Your hand forces your eyes to read faster than your ability to vocalize the words. This lets you read at a visual rather than at a vocal rate.

LESSON ONE: BASIC TECHNIQUES

There are several basic techniques that require you to move your hand across the page as you read. *How* you move your hand in each instance makes the difference.

When you move your hand across the page, you can use one or two fingers. Many people feel comfortable using their index finger. If you are in the habit of using a pen or pencil in your work, you may wish to use it instead. If you want to use a pen, make sure it is capped. If you want to use a pencil, use one that has not been sharpened. Otherwise, you will mark the text. Aside from destroying text, you will distract yourself from the reading and look instead on the marks you are making. Whether you use fingers, a pen, or a pencil, the object that you move across the page is called a *pacer*. We'll use the terms "finger" and "pacer" interchangeably in this book.

Which hand should you use when you are learning to speed-read? Either will work, but most people find it easier and more comfortable to use their *left* hand. Since English is written from left to right, from top to bottom, the left hand is more able to follow this pattern. In addition, it leaves the right hand free for turning pages. If you are right-handed and find it clumsy to use your left hand to scan the page, use your right hand. In any event, take the extra time now to see whether you should use your left hand or right hand to scan the text more easily. If you are not comfortable with the technique, it won't work as efficiently. Let's try it out.

For the purpose of this exercise, assume that you have decided to use your left hand to scan the page and your right hand to turn the page. What about your eyes? Focus them directly above or to the right of your fingers. The only place *not* to focus on is your palm. Whatever you do, do not let your hand motions distract your eye from the page. Experiment to see which focal point is most comfortable. With practice, your eyes and hand will soon be moving smoothly down a page of type. You'll even forget that you have your hand on the page!

Directions

1. Use the pointer and middle fingers of your *left* hand to guide your eyes across the page.
2. Focus your eyes *in front of* your fingers. Read for one minute.

Now try it again, this way:

1. Use the pointer and middle fingers of your *left* hand to guide your eyes across the page.
2. Focus your eyes *above* your fingers. Read for one minute.

Which way was more comfortable? Now try this:

1. Use the pointer and middle fingers of your *right* hand to guide your eyes across the page.
2. Focus your eyes *in front of* your fingers. Read for one minute.

Now try it again, this way:

1. Use the pointer and middle fingers of your *right* hand to guide your eyes across the page.
2. Focus your eyes *above* your fingers. Read for one minute.

Secure Hand Movement

Now let's look at different ways to get your hands and eyes to work together. The first way, the *secure hand movement,* is the most basic technique. It is "secure" because it helps you focus on every line. Even after you learn more difficult hand–eye methods, you may wish to use this simple technique on technical articles and reports that require more concentration.

Using your finger as a guide, trace each line of type from the left margin to the right margin. At the end of the right margin, swing your finger slightly to the right. This will help you prevent sudden stops. Continue the motion even if you come to an incomplete line.

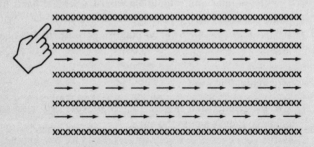

Practice

Practice the secure hand movement on the following passage. Remember to trace each line of type from the left margin to the right margin. Don't forget to swing your finger slightly to the right at the end of a line to help you prevent sudden stops. Continue the motion even if you come to a partial line.

Lightning Strikes Me Again!

Lightning is one of the most dramatic—and dangerous—events in nature. It is also one of the most common. At any every moment of the day, about 2,000 thunderstorms are occurring throughout the world, creating some 100 flashes of lightning. Our fear of Nature's pyrotechnics is understandable, considering their spectacular display. Although most of the 8 million flashes created each day are harmless, about 20 percent produce cloud-to-ground
10 discharges. These are the events that damage property, kill and injure people, and ignite fires. As a matter of fact, lightning is the second leading cause of forest fires—only people start more. Lightning sets off about 50,000 forest fires a year, including 10,000 in America alone.

Not only property is damaged by lightning. About 150 people die every year as a result of being struck by one of these fierce thunderbolts. Around the world, lightning kills more people than any other weather event except floods. That's more than earthquakes, hurricanes, or other natural
20 disasters. Sometimes lighting is so powerful that it can blow off a person's shoe as it surges through the body.

Every country has its myths about lightning. In some areas, certain trees are presumed to repel lightning; others, to attract it. The hawthorn, laurel, aspen, beech, alder, and bay trees are believed by some to repel lightning, while the

poplar, locust, and walnut attract it. Some Americans believe that fires caused by lightning can be put out only by milk. Some people believe that dogs and cats attract lightning. One of the most widespread beliefs about
30 lightning is that it will not strike the same place twice. This is simply not true.

We've come a long way since Ben Franklin tied a key to a kite to find out how lightning works. Today, scientists know that lightning flashes between a positively charged area and a negatively charged one. These can be different parts of the same cloud, different clouds, or a cloud and the earth. Air insulates between these charges, but when the electrical attraction becomes too strong to be contained by the air, it flashes out. Lightning blazes with heat reaching 54,000
40 degrees Fahrenheit or more. That's five times hotter than the sun's atmosphere.

If lightning terrifies you, you can resort to the time-honored tradition of hiding under the bed, or you can move to a different part of the world. Most lightning strikes between 30° N and 30° S. Or try riverboat life, because lightning is ten times more likely to strike over land than over water.

Reading Rate: _____

Semisecure Hand Movement

With this method, you use your pacer to follow just the center portion of a passage. Because you are scanning less type, you can read much more quickly. As a result, this method is far more efficient than the secure hand movement. In fact, it can more than double your reading rate!

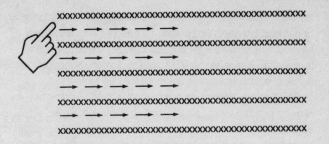

Practice

Practice the semisecure hand movement on the following passage. Remember to trace only the middle of each line of type from the left margin to the right.

Reducing Problems with VDTs

There are a variety of interventions that employers can use to reduce or prevent harmful effects associated with VDT use. Some of them are discussed in the following paragraphs.

Light should be directed so that it does not shine in the operator's eyes when she or he is looking at the screen. Further, lighting should be adequate for the operator to see the text and the screen, but not so bright as to cause glare
10 or discomfort.

There are four basic lighting factors that must be controlled to provide suitable office illumination and avoid eyestrain: quantity, contrast, direct glare, and reflected glare. In most offices, light fixtures and daylight provide illumination for work surfaces. High illumination "washes out" images on the display screen; therefore, if possible, where VDTs are used, illumination levels should be somewhat lower, around

28–50 footcandles. Contrast is the difference in luminance or brightness between two areas. To prevent the visual load
20 caused by alternate light and dark areas, the difference in illumination between the VDT display screen, horizontal work surface, and surrounding areas should be minimized.

Most of the difficulties associated with VDTs do not require precise visual acuity, and indirect lighting is appropriate. The advantages of diffuse lighting are twofold: there tend to be fewer hot spots, or glare sources, in the visual field; and the contrasts created by the shapes of objects tend to be softer. The result, in terms of luminous intensities, is a more uniform visual field. Where indirect
30 lighting is not used, parabolic louvers on overhead lights are probably the next best way to ensure that light is diffused.

Glare is usually defined as a harsh, uncomfortably bright light. It is dependent on the size, intensity, angle of incidence, luminance, and proximity of the source of the line of sight (windows) or reflected light from polished sources (keyboards), or from more diffuse reflections that may reduce contrast (improper task lighting). Glare may cause annoyance, discomfort, or loss of visual performance and
40 visibility.

In many cases, the reorientation of workstations may be all that is necessary to move sources of glare from the line of sight. The proper "treatment" for windows may be baffles, venetian blinds, draperies, shades, or filters. The face of the display screen should be at right angles to windows and light sources. Care should be taken, especially when terminals are installed within 20 feet of windows, to ensure that there is some method of blocking sunlight, such as blinds or curtains.
50 Since light reflects from walls and work surfaces visible

around the screen, these areas should be painted a medium color and have a nonreflective finish. Workstations and lighting should be arranged to avoid reflected glare on the display screen and surrounding surfaces.

Antiglare filters that attach directly to the surface of a VDT screen can help reduce glare. Two types of filters are available: natural density filters, which scatter and diffuse some of the light reflected off the display screen, and micromesh filters, which not only scatter the light but also 60 absorb most of the light reflected from the surface of the screen by means of an embedded interwoven grid of dyed nylon fibers. Newer model keyboards tend to have antiglare matte finishes. Further, lighting should be adequate to enable the operator to see the text and screen, but not so bright as to cause glare. When used, work station lighting should be easily adjustable and directed at source documents, not at the display screen surface.

Reading Rate: _____

The Smooth Hand Movement

With the smooth hand movement, you will bite off even larger units of type. Since this makes comprehension a bit harder, this method is especially useful on easy-to-read material, such as newspapers and magazines. Position your finger at the left-hand margin, under a line of type. Keep your finger on the page as you return to the left margin, but skip under a line or two as you move. This movement may feel awkward at first, but stick with it! Soon it will feel natural, and can greatly increase your reading rate!

Practice

Practice the smooth hand movement on the following passage. Remember to come back to the left a line or two under your former position. Use your pacer to force your eye to move more quickly.

Immigration and America

Immigrants generally come to the United States to work and improve their economic condition, not to collect welfare. A 1985 study by the U.S. Bureau of Labor Statistics found that, contrary to the general expectation, the foreign born do not seem to be more likely than native-born Americans to be receiving government assistance. In contrast, the share of foreign-born people in America collecting government assistance, including unemployment benefits, food stamps,
10 Supplemental Security Income, and Aid to Families with Dependent Children (AFDC) was about 2 percent less than it was for the native-born Americans.

Studies show that after about 15 years of living in America, immigrants earn more than native-born workers, in

general. The result is that most immigrants pay more in taxes over their lifetimes than they receive in government benefits. They pay Social Security taxes during their working years. They often do not have parents in this country collecting benefits, so they create a windfall for other
20 Americans. By the time immigrants collect Social Security themselves, their children are paying into the system.

Further, immigrants do not just take jobs; they create jobs through their own needs. They also create jobs because they tend to start new businesses and help keep American businesses competitive with overseas concerns. Recent U.S. Department of Labor studies bear this out. A 1986 survey of America's most distinguished scholars and teachers found that most believed immigrants have had a very favorable influence on America. This is clearly true in
30 intellectual endeavors: an astonishing share of America's Nobel Prize winners, high school valedictorians, inventors, Ph.D.s, scientists, and engineers are foreign born.

Reading Rate: _____

LESSON TWO: VARIATIONS

As you practice the secure, semisecure, and smooth hand movements, you will see which ones help you read most quickly. There are other variations for you to consider as well.

The first is *Z-ing*. The name describes the shape of the hand motion. In this hand movement, your pacer moves from left to right and then zigs down two or more lines. Clearly, this can save you a great deal of time. Trace your finger over the following diagram to get the feel of this pattern.

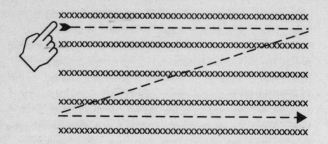

The second variation is *column reading*. With this hand motion, you trace your finger directly down the middle of the page. This is for more accomplished readers. Try it after you have learned the secure, semisecure, and smooth hand movements.

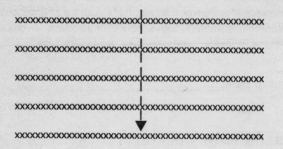

Practice

Practice Z-ing and column reading on this passage. Try half with the first method; half with the second. See which hand motion gives you the better speed.

Matters of Style

Style is fluid, as is language. A style manual must reflect contemporary linguistic transformation in order to be relevant—if language changes, a good style manual must recognize those shifts and incorporate them. *The 21st Century Manual of Style* presents, in one volume, an all-new, authoritative lexical compilation of cutting-edge information and insight regarding all aspects and details of style that are of practical interest to 21st century writers.

10   This computer-age manual tells whether your software is *user friendly* or *user-friendly*. Gender-sensitive entries respect the equality of the sexes in the words we choose, and give the preferred forms of address acceptable for women and men today. The *21st Century Manual of Style* also includes up-to-the-minute names and spellings of the post-Soviet republics and Eastern European nations.

    Entries consisting of new words and advice about their proper spelling and usage (information not yet available in dictionaries) incorporates terms entering the popular culture 20 through business, science, technology, politics, environmentalism, and the arts—from "greenhouse gases" to "Twelve Step" to "glasnost" to "virtual reality," and scores more. Hundreds of the most popular trademarks, and the most prominent companies and corporations, current place-names, titles, and common abbreviations may be accessed by users in seconds.

Reading Rate: _____

The 21st Century Manual of Style distills many contemporary style concerns to produce the innovative style sourcebook writers must have to keep up with the latest developments in 30 the fast-changing world of sound bites.

    The widespread use of personal computers and laser printers has brought publishing capabilities into millions of homes and offices. While technological advances do permit lay people to produce polished documents, the computer has yet to supplant the style sensibility of its user.

The ability to manipulate factors like font and type creates a number of interesting style questions. When are titles set off in quotes? When putting a résumé together, should text be italicized or underscored? What is boldface used for? If
40 you are printing a business report, a flier, your curriculum vitae, or a thesis from a personal computer, you'll find that you can no longer hide behind the stylistic ambiguities a typed or written draft previously afforded you. Your approach to style must be as meticulous, demanding, and current as that of a publishing professional.

When producing a typeset page, matters of style become glaringly obvious; the *21st Century Manual of Style* is designed to help make writers compatible with their computers, enabling desktoppers to produce high-quality,
50 style-conscious documents.

Reading Rate: _____

More Variations

Did you think you were done? Not yet! We've worked out even more reading variations for the 21st century. Our goal? To help you find the one that best suits *your* reading style.

Here are four more ways that you can let your fingers do the walking and really see your reading speed pick up. The first we call the *Bouncing U.* The name describes the bounce at the bottom of the page. Some people trace the entire shape with their left hand, while others begin with the left and pick up with the right at the bottom of the U. Trace over this diagram with your pacer to practice. Try it with both one hand and two hands, to see which variation you find more comfortable.

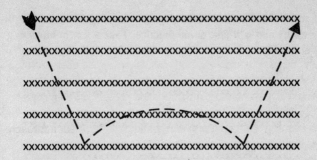

The second variation we call the *V*. No surprises here — the name clearly describes the shape you trace as you speed-read. Again, this variation can be done with one hand or with two. If you use two hands, start at each side and move toward the bottom of the figure. If you want to use one hand, begin at the left column and trace down and up again. You can see by the shape of this figure how much type it can help you digest more quickly. Trace the shape until it feels comfortable for you.

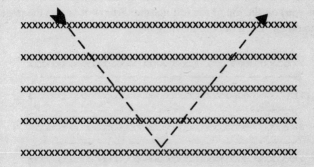

The third variation is *Double Margins*. This is clearly a two-handed variation. Position your left hand on the top of the left margin. Position your right hand on the right margin. Pull both hands down the sides of the page as you read. This one is a little tricky and will take some practice. Take a few minutes to go over it now.

The final variation is one of the all-time winners: We call it *Making Tracks*. You can shorten the track if you are reading difficult text. You can expand it if the text is less challenging. Place your left hand (or right hand, if that is more comfortable for you) on the top of the left margin. Follow it across the page and down. Try it out on this diagram.

It's important to be comfortable when you read. Otherwise, no matter how well you learn these techniques, you will get fatigued easily and slow your pace. Follow these guidelines for maximum results.

---

1. Put the reading material on a table or desk in a comfortable position. Don't read hunched over.
2. Keep your elbows close to your body. This will help prevent your arms from getting tired.
3. Don't move your head from side to side.
4. Don't say any of the words aloud.

What Is Style?

American English is rich and varied. Given the breadth and magnitude of the language, writers often encounter instances of ambiguity when they attempt to express themselves in writing.

Fortunately, a few systems of composition can help to ensure that what is written will be understood. When ideas are transferred from the mind to paper, the rules of grammar must order a writer's thoughts. Efforts to convey the proper meaning are then fine-tuned by paying close attention to stylistic considerations. In writing, "style" refers to the customary practices of spelling, punctuation, capitalization, abbreviation, and typography. The manner in which these elements are employed throughout your writing subtly directs the form and appearance of the completed written piece. Therefore, style considerations greatly impact upon the tone and character of your writing, exercising a profound influence over how your meaning will be received by your reader. The more rigidly a standard of style is observed, the more coherently and exactly your intentions will be translated into text. The less uniformly style standards are respected, the less precise and accurate your writing will become.

Whether composing a novel, a business letter, or a term paper, strive for good style by adhering to a set of guidelines that are consistent, appropriate to the nature of the text, and likely to be familiar to your audience.

Reading Rate: _____

Five Quick Hints for Faster Reading

1. Push Hard

You know your reading speed — now push a little harder. Every day, read a little faster than is comfortable. Set aside a few minutes every day to see how much faster you can read. Time yourself as you learned in Chapter 1.

2. Use Context Clues

Even the best, fastest readers are occasionally stumped by unfamiliar words. Their secret? They guess the meaning of the word by its *context,* the neighboring words. You'll learn more about this later. For now, don't be hung up by new words. Skim over them and keep on reading.

3. Don't Vocalize

One of the reasons why people read slowly is that they say the words aloud as they read. Don't! If you find yourself falling into this habit, suck on a piece of hard candy. It will help you refrain from reading aloud.

4. Cut Down on Distractions

Studies have shown that reading to background music can help you block out distractions. Try playing the radio softly as you read. If this will distract others, use headphones or a headset. Caution! Make sure that the music itself isn't distracting. Stay away from vocal music; stick to instrumentals.

5. Think about What You're Reading

Try to concentrate on the written page and forget about what your eyes are doing.

3

The Eyes Have It: Training Your Eyes to Increase Reading Speed

Before we discuss specific ways to speed up your reading, let's make sure we are all speaking the same language. Here are several terms that reading professionals use to describe the reading process. As you go through this book, you will learn how these terms relate to faster, more accurate reading.

Rapid Reading Terms

Fixations: the way your eyes pause on certain words and letters. Fixations slow your reading because they interrupt the flow of the text.

Regressions: moving your eyes backward to reread specific lines. At the end of a regression is a fixation, as your eyes zero in on specific words or letters.

Return sweeps: the smooth flow of your eyes from one line of type to the next. The better your return sweeps, the more quickly you will read.

Span of perception: the number of letters or symbols you can perceive in a single sweep. The larger your span of perception, the more type you can take in at one glance. The more type you can perceive, the more quickly you can read.

Span of recognition: the number of letters or symbols you can perceive and *understand* in a single sweep. The span of recognition describes reading comprehension as well as perception. Rapid reading is not just seeing more type. Your reading will not improve if you just see the letters; you must be able to interpret the words as well.

How does the reading process work, using these terms? You begin reading a passage with **fixation,** as your eyes focus on the first word. Your eyes take in groups of letters, your **span of perception,** as you read through the text. If you are reading smoothly, there will be quick **return sweeps,** as you progress from line to line. After training, you will know how to cut down on **regressions** to increase your **span of recognition,** and thus your reading speed.

LESSON ONE: SPAN OF PERCEPTION

Let's start by checking your span of perception. Read the following five passages to see which is the *easiest* for you to read. Read at a comfortable pace. Then rate the passages from easiest to hardest.

Passage 1

Animals   talk   to   each   other,   of   course.   There
can   be   no   question   about   that;   but   I   suppose

there are very few people who can understand them. I never knew but one man who could. He was a middle-aged, simple-hearted miner who had lived in a lonely corner of California, among the woods and mountains, a good many years, and had studied the ways of his only neighbors, the beasts and the birds, until he believed he could accurately translate any remark they made. This was Jim Baker. According to Jim Baker, some animals have only a limited education, and use only very simple words, and scarcely ever a comparison or a flowery figure; whereas certain other animals have a very large vocabulary, a fine command of language and a ready and fluent delivery. Consequently these latter talk a great deal; they like it; they are conscious of their talent, and they enjoy showing off. Baker said that after a long and careful observation, he had come to the conclusion that the bluejays were the best talkers among birds and beasts.

Passage 2

Though really a good-hearted, good-tempered old fellow at bottom, yet he is singularly fond of being in the midst of contention. It is one of his peculiarities, however, that he only relishes the beginning of an affray; he always goes into a fight with alacrity, but comes out of it grumbling even when victorious; and though no one fights with more obstinacy to carry a contested point, yet, when the battle is over, he comes to the reconciliation and is so much taken up with the mere

shaking of   hands that   he is   apt to   let his
antagonists pocket   all that   they have   been quarreling
about. It   is not,   therefore, fighting   that he   ought so
much to   be on   his guard   against, as   making friends.
He is   like a   stout ship,   which will   weather the
roughest storm   uninjured, but   roll its   masts overboard
in the   succeeding calm.

Passage 3

Who will be   the new managers?   They won't be
the old hands-on   factory bosses of   yesteryear, and they
won't be the   slash-and-burn   masters of the
last decade. Rather,   they will be   globalists, part of
the entire world,   not attached to   any one small
piece. They will   be able to   marshal disparate forces,
and move among   markets with fluid   ease. Able to
network-manage, they   will make horizontal
alliances rather than   traditional hierarchical orderings.
They will clearly   understand information technology.
The head honcho   will agitate for   a highly skilled
work force and   skill development. A   hands-on leader and
a conceptualist, the   new chief will   have equal ability
to exploit information   technology and stay   in touch with
outlets. Both humble   and brash, the   new managers will
suppress ego while   simultaneously initiating bold
business strategies.

Passage 4

When memory chips become   even less expensive, we
will be able to   put more memory into
computers so they can   understand what they are
capable of doing. Then,   for example, the new

intelligent tools of the   home—VCRs, home appliances,
kitchen equipment—will be   operated by voice commands.
The greatest challenge will   be to integrate all
these products electronically. We   will need an industry
standard, what is called   a bus system, to
send the signals that   will connect everything in
the home. Then you   could control everything by
one hand-held unit   or by the telephone
outside the house. You   might make one call
to heat your bath,   for example, or one   to turn on the
oven or cool the   house. These things are
technically possible now, but   they will not become
a reality until there   are worldwide standards. All
the big electronics companies   are discussing how to
do this.

Passage 5

A publishing system   is not a single technology
or piece of hardware,   but a synthesis of
computers, input devices, output devices, and software.
The system may consist of   a personal computer,
mouse, laser   printer, and publishing software,
or be a conglomeration of   personal computers,
workstations,   minicomputers, CAD systems,
scanners, laser printers,   typesetters, CD-Rom
devices, and software.   Users   have the ability to
tie different types of computers together   and/or
purchase the system components   from different vendors
as their system needs   evolve or
as new products emerge.   However,   this freedom
to mix and match   systems and peripherals
can create   configuration nightmares   such as
incompatible hardware   and/or software,

nonworking systems, or systems
that produce erroneous results.

If you are already a good reader, you would find the *last* one
the easiest to read; the first, the most difficult. The one that
seems to be the most comfortable to you indicates the size of
your span of perception. As you increase your span of perception, you may wish to review these passages from time to time.

Increasing Perception Span

Now it is time to increase your span of perception. The greater
your span of perception, the more quickly you will be able to
read. There are several ways to stretch your span of perception.
Among the easiest ways is the following exercise.

Most people can see a four-digit number at a glance and
remember it long enough to write it down or say it aloud. In
this exercise, you will begin with a single-digit number and
work up to a six-digit one. Use your index finger to guide your
eye from asterisk to asterisk. With the other hand, write down
the number on a separate sheet of paper. Or you can just say
the number aloud. Try to work as quickly as possible.

Exercise

*

3

*

7

*

4

*

9

*

2
*
5
*
1
*
6
*
33
*
14
*
17
*
29
*
43
*
88
*
71
*
54
*
62
*
982
*
865
*
430
*
189
*

395
*
211
*
371
*
555
*
900
*
3864
*
4463
*
1192
*
1234
*
8628
*
3711
*
4566
*
2881
*
6615
*
44328
*
56891
*
26789
*
67113

*

95277

*

63678

*

33167

*

93001

*

66781

*

556211

*

431178

*

458890

*

212256

*

567110

*

035601

*

431567

*

842156

*

125678

Focus on Words

Let's expand what you have learned to focus your span of perception on words. When you look at one word, you focus directly on it, like this:

pumpernickel

When you see two words, you should focus in the middle of the two. Try these:

read fast
operating system
laser printer

The same is true of groups of three words—you should keep your eyes focused in the middle. The difficulty arises with larger groups of words. You know that the more type you can process at a time, the more quickly you can read. *Fixations* slow your reading because they interrupt the flow of the text. *Regressions* cost you even more time. How can you stretch your *span of perception* and *span of recognition?* The trick is to train your eye to keep the focus on the middle of the word group.

Exercise

Use this exercise to train your eye and brain to expand your perception and recognition spans. Use your index finger to guide your eyes. Work as quickly as you can, and be sure to keep the focus on the middle of the word group.

private
*
company
*
modules
*
commercial
*
venture
*

contracts
*

president
*

commencement
*

remove
*

agencies
*

private eye
*

high degree
*

light waves
*

leather jacket
*

Chinese porcelain
*

plain countenance
*

finance capital
*

informational interview
*

modernistic sculpture
*

graphics capability
*

adequate work space
*

streamlined office environment
*

height and distance
*

normal work surface
*

Department of Labor
*

General Administration Building
*

International Newspaper Guild
*

video display terminals
*

user-friendly computers
*

state plan designers
*

Department of Industrial Relations
*

occupational safety and health
*

Department of Licensing and Regulation
*

Health and Environment Bureau
*

Communication Workers of America
*

Centers for Disease Control
*

hazard prevention and control
*

private and public administrations
*

improved quality of content
*

reader impact and impression
*

disseminate information in electronic form
*

improved integrity and confidentiality control
*

exchange data between different computers
*

growing cost of producing documents
*

printing volume of the office
*

increased typographic control and composition
*

supporting several different output devices
*

conversion software or import filters
*

international federal standards of shipping
*

personal computer, mouse, laser printer
*

involve multiple people and related organizations
*

topmost line of the point-of-purchase display
*

undergo extensive review and revision cycles
*

how well the function is performed
*

system integrator must configure the system
*

manually place and adjust the document
*

high-resolution monitor that formats
*

sufficient memory in the computer system
*

evaluation matrix is a comprehensive listing
*

understanding the requirements, capabilities, and limitations
*

LESSON TWO: READING KEY WORDS IN THE 21ST CENTURY

Once you have widened your recognition and perception spans, it's time to take a look at reading key words. This technique is best suited for instances when you do *not* want to read an article thoroughly, when your primary goal is a quick overview of the contents. Here's what you do.

Run your eyes over the article in a fast zigzag motion. As your eyes pick up important words, stop and read that section in more depth. You will be training your eyes to stop at the most important points, using key words as your tip-off.

Try it with the following article. As you read it quickly, try to locate the key words. Stop there briefly, and then move on.

Fly Right

All pilots except those flying gliders and free air balloons must possess valid medical certificates in order to exercise the privileges of their pilots' licenses. The periodic medical examinations required for medical certification are conducted by the designated aviation medical examiners, who are physicians with a special interest in aviation safety and training in aviation medicine.

Even a minor illness suffered in day-to-day living can seriously degrade performance of many piloting tasks vital to safe flight. Illness can produce fever and distracting symptoms that can impair judgment, memory, alertness, and the ability to make calculations. Although symptoms from an illness may be under adequate control with a medication, the medication itself may decrease pilot performance.

The safest rule is not to fly while suffering from any illness. If this rule is considered too stringent for a particular illness, the pilot should contact an aviation medical examiner for advice.

Pilot performance can be seriously degraded by both prescription and over-the-counter medications, as well as by the medical conditions for which they are taken. Many medications, such as tranquilizers, sedatives, pain relievers, and cough-suppressant preparations, have primary effects that may impair judgment, memory, alertness, coordination, vision, and the ability to make calculations. Any medication that depresses the nervous system, such as a sedative, tranquilizer, or antihistamine, can make a pilot much more susceptible to hypoxia.

Here are some of the key words you might have located:
    medical certificates
    fever
    alertness
    medications
    symptoms
    decrease
    nervous system
    medical examinations
    impair judgment
    not to fly
    hypoxia

Exercise

Now locate the key words on your own in the following article. Remember to keep your eyes swinging over less important text and focus on the key words. Keep track of the time so you can calculate your reading rate at the end.

Knowledge Viewed in Relation to Professional Skill

Now this is what some great people are very slow to allow; they insist that education should be confined to some particular and narrow end, and should issue in some definite work, which can be weighed and measured. They argue as if every thing, as well as every person, has its price; and that where there has been a great outlay, they have a right to expect a return in kind. This they call making education and instruction "useful," and "utility" becomes their watchword.

10 With a fundamental principle of this nature, they very naturally go on to ask what there is to show for the expense of a university; what is the real worth in the market of the article called "a liberal education," on the supposition that it does not teach us definitely how to advance our manufacturers, or to improve our lands, or to better our civil economy. Or again, if it does not at once make this person a lawyer, that an engineer, and that a surgeon; or at least if it does not lead to discoveries in chemistry, astronomy, geology, magnetism, and science of every kind.

20 This question, as might have been expected, has been keenly debated in the present age, and formed one main subject of the controversy among people of all ranks and backgrounds. I say, let us take "useful" to mean not what is simply good, what *tends* to be good, or is the instrument of good; and in this sense also, I will show you how a liberal education is truly and fully a useful thing, although it be not a professional education. "Good" indeed means one thing, and

"useful" means another; but I lay it down as a principle,
which will save us a good deal of anxiety, that, although the
30 useful is not always good, the good is always useful. Good is
not only good but it fosters good; this is one of its attributes.
Nothing is excellent, beautiful, perfect, desirable in its own
sake, but it overflows, and spreads the likeness of itself all
around it. Good is prolific; it is not only good to the eye but to
the taste; it not only attracts us, but it communicates itself; it
excites first our admiration and love, then our desire and
gratitude, and that is in proportion to our intenseness and
fullness in particular instances. A great good will impart great
good. If, then, the intellect is so excellent a portion of us, and
40 its cultivation so excellent, it is not only perfect in itself, but in
a true and high sense it must be useful to the possessor and
to all around him; not useful in any low, mechanical,
mercantile sense, but as diffusing good, or as a blessing, or
a gift, or power, or treasure, first to the owner, and through
the owner to the world. I say, then, if a liberal education be
good, it must necessarily be useful too.

Reading rate: _____

LESSON THREE: PHRASE READING

Enlarging your perception and recognition spans is so important to super speed-reading that experts have worked out still
other techniques for mastering this skill. Here's another
method to help you shave off precious seconds of reading time.

Phrase reading will help you reduce the number of times
your eyes stop and start. By taking in bigger chunks of type,
you'll save significant reading time. Read this sentence for a
sample of what we mean:

The   1980s   witnessed   an   increasing
awareness   of   the   potential   economic
value   of   space.

How long did it take you to read that sentence? Too long!
That's because your eye stopped at every single word.
  Now try it again:

The 1980s witnessed an increasing awareness of the
potential economic value of space.

Faster, right? Why? Think about how we construct meaning
from what we read. Meaning does not come from every single
word but from the sum of those words taken together. It's only
when you put the words together that they make sense. As a
result, the reader who sees words in units is already ahead of
the reader who visualizes individual words. The second sentence made much more sense than the first because you read
the words as interconnected groups, not as single words. By
reading groups of words, you read faster because you cut the
number of times your eyes stop on the page. You also understand more because you're reading in terms of ideas and
thoughts rather than in terms of individual words.
  A big part of phrase reading is *rereading.* Everyone rereads
confusing passages, but beware of needless rereading. If you
don't understand a passage, you have to go back over it. But
many readers have gotten into the habit of rereading a line even
though they have understood it. This wastes a great deal of
time and can really slow your pace. If you recognize that
you're guilty of this time-wasting habit, practice a smooth eye
motion. Keep aware of the tendency to reread needlessly. Stop
yourself when you see you're doing it.
  Here's a practice passage to try out this technique.
Underline the phrases as you read.

Practice

Diamonds Are Forever

Diamonds are the most valuable stones on earth. They are formed of pure carbon and are the hardest substance known to humanity.

They are thought to be the most beautiful of all the gems, but through the ages many people have felt fearful and jittery about them to the point of irrational superstition. Perhaps this is due to the way diamonds were created. They were born deep within the earth under exceptional pressure. Volcanoes
10 threw them to the surface in streams of fire and melted rock.

Some of them never reached the open air. They fell and stuck to the sides of the volcano's tunnel. Diamond mines are nothing more than worn-out volcano tunnels, called *pipes* by the miners.

Most of today's diamonds come from South Africa, but the first large diamond mines were in India many centuries ago. It was from these mines that many of the most famous—or infamous?—diamonds originated. Rumor has it that some of them have brought bad luck to their owners.

Reading time: _____

S-t-r-e-t-c-h M-o-r-e

Here's another way to stretch your span of perception. Read through these entries from the telephone book as fast as you can, guiding your eyes with an index card. Then answer the questions that follow.

Corey Coffee Services 138 Toledo, Bthpg	256-8854
Corwin L 1A Hazel Av, Frmdgl	753-0191
Corzane Cabinet Makers 55 Allen Blvd, E Medw	822-9181

Cosajay Mario 27 Barbara, No Masspqua	867-7633
Cosby Andrew 40 Alexander Ave, Seafrd	420-0191
Cosenza A 315 Hicksville Rd, Bthpg	293-4981
Consgriff JH 239 10th, E Medw	731-3311
Coskie Scott 12 Keith La Frmdgl	420-9877
Cosmo Anthony 4672 Lincoln Av Hunt Sta	271-7731
Cosmo Limousine Service 98 Main St, Patchg	657-3333
Cosmos Electric Mach Corp 140 Schmidt Blvd, Bthpg	410-5421
Cost Plus, Inc. 44 Millbar, E Medw	822-7761
Costa Louise 18 Sullivan Ave, Hunt	351-9889

Questions

1. What is the address for Mario Cosajay?_____

   _____

2. What business do the people at 55 Allen Boulevard have?

   _____

   _____

3. What is the telephone number for Andrew Cosby? _____

   _____

4. Where could you get supplies for your coffeemaker? __

   _____

   _____

5. Where does Louise Costa live? _____

   _____

6. What is the telephone number for A Cosenza?

   _____

Answers

1. 27 Barbara, No Masspqua
2. They are cabinetmakers.
3. 420-0191
4. Corey Coffee Services
5. 18 Sullivan Ave, Hunt
6. 293-4981

LESSON FOUR: SPACE READING FOR THE FUTURE

How did you do? What adjustments did you make in your field of vision to take in more than one word at a time? One of the best ways to train your eyes to grasp entire phrases is through *space reading.* Rather than looking right at the words, lift your eyes so they focus a little bit above the line. Then allow your eyes to relax slightly and spread your vision over more than one word at a time. This will help you read entire groups of words together. Here's an example of phrases cut out from the previous passage:

the most valuable stones on earth
formed of pure carbon
hardest substances known
the most beautiful of all the gems
through the ages
felt fearful and jittery
to the point of irrational superstition
due to the way
diamonds were created
deep within the earth
under exceptional pressure
Volcanoes threw them to the surface

in streams of fire and melted rock
the open air
stuck to the sides
worn-out volcano tunnels
from South Africa
in India many centuries ago
some of them
brought bad luck to their owners

Notice that these are not just any phrases—they are *meaningful* ones. As you read, look for units of thought. As you read the rest of this book, underline meaningful phrases.

How can you find these phrases? Hold an index card in your dominant hand as you read. Move the card down the page at a faster-than-normal rate. Vary the rate until you feel comfortable. Then try to speed it up gradually, moving the card faster down the page. Ask a friend to check your eye movements to see if you are taking in single words or whole phrases. You can also do the same exercise using the hand motions described in Chapter 2.

Here's a practice passage to try out this technique.

Practice

NASA Today

Today, NASA is providing a focus for action to expand U.S. private-sector investment and involvement in the civilian space program. The agency established the Office of Commercial Programs to actively support new, high-tech space ventures, the commercial application of existing aeronautics and space technology, and commercial access to available NASA capabilities and services. This role is strengthened by NASA's rich tradition of cooperation with
10 industry.

The roots of U.S. dedication to space leadership are contained in the National Aeronautics and Space Act of 1958. A key national objective, spelled out in NASA's charter, is "the preservation of the United States as a leader in aeronautical and space science technology and in the application thereof to the conduct of peaceful activities within and outside the atmosphere."

Reading time: _____

Try it again with a more challenging passage.

Exercise

Work

For there is a perennial nobleness, and even sacredness, in work. There is always hope in a person who actually and earnestly works; in idleness is there perpetual despair. Work, never so mean, *is* in communication with nature; the real desire to get work done will itself lead one more and more to truth, to nature's appointments and regulations that are truth.

The latest gospel in this world is, know your work and do it. "Know yourself": long enough has that poor "self" of yours
10 tormented you; you will never get to "know" it, I believe! Think it not your business, this of knowing yourself; you are an unknowable individual; know what you can work at, and work at it, like a Hercules! That will be your better plan.

It has been written, "An endless significance lies in work"; people perfect themselves by working. Foul jungles are cleared away, fair fields rise instead, and stately cities; and withal the person ceases to be a jungle and foul, unwholesome desert thereby. Consider how, even in the meanest sorts of labor, the whole soul of a person is
20 composed into a kind of real harmony, the instant the person

sets to work! Doubt, desire, sorrow, remorse, indignation, despair itself—all these like hell dogs beleaguer the soul of the poor day worker, as of every person; but when people bend themselves with free valor against their tasks, all these are stilled, all these shrink murmuring far off into their caves. The person is now a person. The blessed glow of labor in him or her, is it not purifying fire, wherein all poison is burned up, and of sour smoke itself there is made bright blessed flame!

30   Destiny, on the whole, has no other way of cultivating us. A formless chaos, once set revolving, grows round and ever rounder; ranges itself, by mere force of gravity, into strata, spherical courses; is no longer chaos, but a round, compacted world. What would become of the Earth, did it cease to revolve? In the poor old Earth, as long as it revolves, all inequalities, irregularities, disperse themselves; all irregularities are incessantly becoming regular. Of an idle, unrevolving person, the kindest destiny, like the most assiduous potter without a wheel, can bake and knead

40 nothing other than a botch; let the potter spend on the clay what expensive coloring, what gilding, and enameling is wished, it is but a botch. Not a dish, no, a bulging, crooked, shambling, amorphous blotch—a mere enameled vessel of dishonor! Let the idle think of this.

Reading time: _____

LESSON FIVE: INDENTATION

Amazingly, people spend as much as *25 percent* of their time reading margins! You can save precious reading time by learning how to read words, not empty space!

When you start reading a line of type, you tend to make your first eye fixation on the first word of the first line. You follow the same pattern at the end of the line. As a result, you make your last eye fixation on the last word of the last line. Since you have already learned that you have a specific span of perception — and it can be increased — it makes sense that if you fixate on the first word of a line, half your vision space is in the margin. This is blank space! What a waste of time!

To read more efficiently, it makes sense to begin several words into the line, not at the margin. In a similar way, it makes sense to stop reading several words before the end of the line, not at the last word. Therefore, make your first eye fixation two or three words into the line, and your last eye fixation two or three words before the end of the line. Never skip words, and focus only on words — not on the margin. If you focus your span of perception an inch or two in from each side of the page, you will be able to adjust your focus.

Here is a sample passage for you to use to train your eyes. We have drawn two vertical lines down the page to show you where to focus.

Computers and Gender

A federally funded study to encourage girls' use of computers, conducted by the Women's Action Alliance, a national nonprofit organization furthering equality for women, illustrated some differences in learning styles. The study, entitled "The Neuter Computer: Computers for Boys and Girls," concluded: "while many boys seem to enjoy the computer for its own sake—playing around with it just to see what it can do—many girls seem to value the computer for
10 how it can help them do what they want or have to do. In other words, computers are often a means for girls but an end for boys." The same study also found that seventh- and

eighth-grade boys are far more likely than girls to use the computer in school during free time and more likely to have a home computer and to use it.

Hoping to reduce the disparity, the Women's Action Alliance, funded by the National Science Foundation, is sponsoring a computer-equity project involving six school districts in New York State. One of these districts started a
20 computer club just for girls. The girls like to select their own computer projects, instead of the militaristic, competitive games usually selected by the boys, according to the results. Once the girls develop more confidence about using computers, they are most likely to take part in joint computer projects with boys.

Recent evidence indicates that gender-related differences in attitudes toward computers and technology continue through adulthood, even among those who use computers in their careers.

Reading rate: _____

Exercise

Now try it yourself without the guidelines. Use this passage, and focus your span of perception about one inch into each column.

Electronic Publishing Issues

To select and effectively manage the publishing system, it is necessary to examine and understand the technological, managerial, and design issues related to publishing. The issues presented are general in nature, pertaining to principles and directions. An explanation of each issue is followed by a discussion of some of the current and potential

ways of dealing with it. The list of issues, though not
exhaustive, contains many of the more salient concerns with
10 respect to choosing and operating a publishing system.

Information Integration

Basic to electronic publishing is the ability to integrate
different types of information into a single document. The
information, whether it be character, graphic, tabular, or
mathematical, may be created on a variety of text and graphic
systems. The different text formatters, graphics drawing
packages, CAD systems, and scanner software have their own
conventions for representing data, formatting instructions, and
organizing the structural relationships among components.
20 This variety of representations presents an obstacle to
integration. The publishing system must be able to understand
the different data formats, and either manage them or
incorporate the information into its own internal data format.

Currently, we deal with incompatible data formats by
using converters or filters to translate the information into a
form understood by the publishing software. These
converters may be an integral part of the publishing software
or available separately from the vendor or third-party
vendors. However, this method of converting formats may be
30 inadequate and uneconomical because

- The appropriate conversion software is not available
- The conversion software does not handle graphics
- The conversion process may cause some loss of data
  and format information
- The conversion process may be cumbersome, requiring
  several steps before the information is in the appropriate
  format.

One solution to overcoming the conversion problem is to
provide an information interchange mechanism that is

40 independent of any system, device, application, or data. Standards are such a mechanism. Using standards, information can be effectively shared among dissimilar systems and integrated together. Moreover, the quality and consistency of the information are assured. One standard, commonly referred to as ODA, provides for the representation and encoding of text and graphic information so that it can be transferred between different systems irrespective of their manufacturer.

50 Until implementations of ODA are readily available, conversion and import filters will continue to be the method of achieving information integration. To ensure a successful conversion, one in which your information is understood by the publishing system:

1. Consider the type of information you use and its data formats
2. Determine if conversion software or import filters are available for these formats from the publishing software vendor
3. Evaluate the effectiveness of the converter or filter.

Reading rate: _____

LESSON SIX: READING IN COLUMNS

When you feel comfortable reading indented sections of text, it's time to learn how to read in columns. When added to what you have already learned, this technique can really speed up your reading. Here's how you do it.

When you read a line of type, your eyes do not travel in a single smooth line. Instead, they move with a series of stops

and starts. These are called *eye fixations*. The more your eyes
stop, the longer it will take you to read. Clearly, it's time to get
those eyes moving!

Start with a column of text from a newspaper or magazine.
Draw a line down the middle of the text. As you read, focus
your eyes on the line. *Read each line with a single fixation.*
That way, your span of perception will enlarge even further.

Below is a sample column marked for you. Read the column
as quickly as possible, keeping your eyes focused on the line as
much as you can.

Practice

The Start of the Art

Some early information-distillation
technologies are already available. To
research this article, I used the modem of
my home computer to access electronic
"slipping files." Every morning I dialed onto
CompuServe Information Service, and read
articles on information technology covered
on the news wire services and in several
major newspapers.

Later, I accessed the Computer Library,
an electronic data base housing nearly
50,000 articles about computer technology.
To begin, I located over 500 articles that
mentioned the key word "newspaper." I
reduced the citations by half by finding out
how many of these also mentioned the
word "computers." To narrow down the file
even further, I asked how many articles also
included the word "future." This brought the

total below 100. I scanned the abstracts
and compiled a list of 65 articles to skim.

I also called up IQuest, a data base
connected to similar data bases that include
most magazines written in English,
corporate and government reports, medical
information, the entire Library of Congress
catalog, and an additional 50 newspapers—
including *Pravda!*

What's the downside of this fabulous
technology? It's fabulously expensive.
Certain data bases can cost as much as
$300 per hour to access. This issue has
larger social ramifications. We already know
that those without money have less access
to quality information than those with
money. A poor student, for example, is
more than four times less likely than an
affluent one to have access to a computer.
Will this unequal access to information
create a social divide?

Exercise

The following column of type does not have a line drawn
through it. Visualize the line drawn down the middle of the
page to help you keep your eyes focused. Try to read as
quickly and accurately as you can by taking in larger bites of
type.

Over the next 10 years, the quantity of
information on a computer chip will increase
by a factor of 1,000 or more. This will drive
down the cost of personal computers and

make them very fast, like a super
turbocharged, 10-cylinder racing-car
engine. It will also make computers easier
to use, the way that automatic transmission
made driving a car much easier. In addition,
10 fiber-optic networks will force
communication costs even lower.

In its present form, the PC will never be
a household staple like the telephone or the
television set. The problem is that a home
PC is not part of a network, like a phone or
a TV set. But with fiber-optic technology,
telephones will connect the PC into a
network. When the telephone, TV, and PC
are all connected, the new device will have
20 enormous potential as a household product.

The center of activity for the next 10
years will be this integration of digital, audio,
and video technology with the PC. By the
21st century, portable PCs will be capable
of two-way communications via satellites
and more complex cellular radio networks.

Reading rate: _____

4

Words, Words, Words: Using Speed-Reading Techniques Within Text!

LESSON ONE: READING MORE THAN ONE LINE AT ONCE

Most of us read one line of text at a time. Imagine how much reading speed you can pick up if you can read two or even three lines of type at a time! You can — all it takes is a little practice.

Hold this book about three feet away from your eyes. What do you notice? You can't make out the words, but you can see the shape of the lines. When you read more than one line of type at a time, you're looking for these patterns. You're forcing your eyes to change the way they look at text. To help you take in larger bites of type, increase the speed of your hand motions across the page. This will force your eyes to move more quickly. Try this technique out. Here's how:

1. Read the following passage, one line at a time, for three minutes. Stop and record your progress. Calculate how many words you read.
2. Keep reading for three more minutes, two lines at a time. Stop and record your progress. Calculate how many words you read.
3. Keep reading for three more minutes, three lines at a time. Stop and record your progress. Calculate how many words you read.

Practice this technique as often as you can, taking in larger and larger groups of lines each time. Work up to taking in an entire paragraph in one glance. The following speech, "Toward the 21st Century: An Agenda for Action," was delivered at a recent commencement. Be sure to record your reading speed at the end of the passage.

Toward the 21st Century: An Agenda for Action

American colleges have less than a decade to prepare for the challenges of the 21st century. What can colleges do to prepare students for what is certain to be the most competitive and high-tech society the world has ever known? The challenges to our society have never been greater.

We have a tidal wave of new learners headed for higher education: the Nintendo generation. These students live and breathe technology. They grew up with Atari, Sega, Nintendo, 10 and arcades. These students are accustomed to bold images, fast hand–eye coordination, and instant feedback. Their lives have been made simpler by fax machines, car telephones, call waiting, MTV, and compact disk players. How will universities sustain their interest in higher education? How will they find stimulating and useful work environments? Perhaps it is time to reexamine the ways we teach and deliver instruction. As more technology finds its

way into higher education, we have to look for the skills we
will need in the future. Let's start with technology itself.

20   When it comes to technology in education, "It's hard to
use a crystal ball because the technology is changing every
eighteen months," according to a coordinator for computer
services at a major university. Still, we can make a few
predictions about changes that will affect us all.

At the heart of education's technological transformation is
the *computer,* an information-processing and -transferring
engine comprising several components, including working
and storage memories, video displays, and input devices.
One measure of computer processing power is MIP (millions
30 of instructions per second). Some of the personal computers
used in businesses have about 20 MIPs as against
educational computers' measly 1, and 100 MIP computers
are expected in a few years. We can look forward to more
powerful and less expensive computers, which will put these
tools within the reach of far more people.

The physical form of computers is also evolving, with
notebook and hand-held computers becoming more
common. Eventually, computers may be integrated into
every student's and teacher's desk top. Most likely, the
40 computer's decreasing size and weight will enable students
and teachers to travel from class to class with their own
personal computers.

Notebook computers—battery-powered computers the
size of a purse— can store as much as 60 megabytes (60
million characters of data) in a magnetic hard disk the size of
a wallet. That's the equivalent of about 30,000 book pages.
Researchers predict that within a few years, notebook
computers may store hundreds of megabytes of data on
rewritable optical disks that look like audio CDs. And they
50 may be able to tap huge pools of information by plugging
into a university's network as easily as you would plug a

telephone into an outlet, or by using cellular and radio-frequency modems.

Critical to the future of educational technology is the *network,* a system of plastic and glass fiber-optic cables, copper wiring, radio, microwave, and satellite technologies that serve as a vast data highway. This system will enable students and teachers to retrieve articles, video clips, slides, photographs, and sound recordings from a central resource
60 library. Using two-way video, classes and individual instructors will see and interact with others across the campus—or across the nation. Clearly, this is easier to achieve in the public school system than in a university, especially in those Florida districts that are expanding due to population influx. By the end of 1993, for example, all 180 schools in Florida's Broward County school district will be linked in a vast computer network. With 161,000 elementary and secondary students and 180,000 adult education students, Broward is the eighth largest school district in the
70 nation.

According to an article entitled "The Technology of Tomorrow" that appeared in a recent issue of the *New York Times,* the National Science Foundation is planning to establish a high-speed national fiber-optic network by the year 2000 that will connect all American universities and, perhaps, most secondary schools. Schools using such a network could draw information from virtually any university library in the nation. Some schools are already experimenting with wireless networks that send data via low-
80 power radio waves, and other schools are being designed with network cables built in. Clearly, wireless networks are more flexible than wired ones, but they also are more expensive. Nonetheless, Apple Computer has applied to the Federal Communications Commission for permission to use part of the radio band for wireless computer

communications, suggesting that the field may become
more popular and affordable.

Schools may someday have video wallpaper, images
surrounding students. The key is interactive technology,
90 which enables students and teachers to participate in the
display of information. The video monitor will probably be
connected to computers, video camcorders, videocassette
recorders, laser disks, compact disk players, cable TV,
satellite dishes, and even other classrooms for live, two-way
broadcasts. Eventually, high-definition television using digital
signals will bring photographic-quality images to viewers,
along with computer graphics and data.

The development of satellite receiving dishes the size of
hubcaps will eventually allow homes and individual
100 classrooms to pull in signals from satellites. Using portable
satellite transmitting stations, professors will be able to beam
lectures directly from remote archaeological sites to schools,
and students on field trips can send in on-site reports.

Once the stuff of science fiction, virtual reality is now a
serious topic of educational research. Using virtual reality,
students can "travel" to distant locations and sense that they
are physically present anywhere from Alaska to Hawaii.
They do this by moving through an artificial environment,
wearing a specially wired helmet or goggles, by gesturing
110 with a special glove, and by moving their eyes. Medical
students could hone their skills on virtual patients, for
example, and technology students could build virtual
automobiles.

"One of the positive effects of technology on education
will be to teach people to learn, rather than to learn specific
facts," says David Nagle, head of the Advanced Technology
Group at Apple Computer. The role of teachers, adds Mr.
Nagle, is not diminished but, rather, enhanced by these
technologies, making it worthwhile to spend as much time

120 teaching teachers to use the technologies as teaching students to learn.

Information Technology and Its Impact on American Education, a report commissioned by the U.S. House of Representatives, presents four key questions that offer guidelines for planning educational policies that need to be developed to prepare learners—and professors—to cope with a rapidly changing world:

1. What needs to be learned?
2. Who needs to learn it?
130 3. Who will provide it?
4. How will it be provided and paid for?

We must remain diligent in dealing with changes for tomorrow and not be immobilized by trying to polish the aged mosaics of past practices. We must bear in mind possible educational futures to be sought because of their value to learners everywhere.

First, schooling must be developed with an awareness of the flow of technology and social trends that will require substantial changes in curriculum and instruction. With the 140 prospect of living longer, more older Americans will require post-retirement jobs. Also to be considered are the challenges facing younger workers who must cope with the increasing information glut.

Second, future-oriented school staffs must include people familiar with microelectronic equipment, such as computers and interactive videos.

Third, professors must have an awareness of the diversity of needs among students of varying ages and backgrounds. They must be trained with insights into the differences in the 150 cultures of various ethnic groups and their languages and history, for the demographics of the country are changing.

Demographer Ben Wattenberg recently told reporters that

"This is the first universal nation." Wattenberg said that there is a big difference between living in a nation that is 90 percent white—as was the case in 1980—and living in a nation that is 65 percent nonwhite—as will be the case by the 21st century. The 1990 census confirms the changing composition of America. The country is experiencing large growth in black, Hispanic, and Asian populations and a
160 sharp drop in the white birthrate. Blacks and Hispanics in particular have dramatically increased their numbers.

As we rapidly approach the new millennium, it is imperative that we develop our foresight with regard to new designs and creative innovations for education. Only in this way can we move from isolation to membership in the global community. To this task, we must bring sincerity and action rather than mere talk. Through education, we will have an infinitely better chance to defend our planet against problems such as pollution, resource depletion, excess population growth, and
170 other global threats.

Reading one line at a time:
Number of words _____

Reading two lines at a time:
Number of words _____

Reading three lines at a time:
Number of words _____

LESSON TWO: FINDING TOPIC SENTENCES

You probably found that as you increased the number of lines you scanned at a time, your comprehension decreased. Perhaps you even found yourself rereading sentences or passages to figure out things you might have missed. This is not unusual. With practice, you will find that as you learn to take in more lines of type at a time, your comprehension will pick up. In the meantime, here's a simple, easy way to speed up that process. You'll be amazed at the results.

Specific sentences will tip you off to the contents of a passage. By focusing on those key sentences, you will be able to figure out how to adjust your reading speed to pick up the most information in the least possible time. Finding these sentences will show you where to spend the most time reading, and where to spend the least time.

What types of sentences are you looking for? *Topic sentences.* The topic sentence is the statement that explains the contents of the paragraph. Topic sentences are *general statements* of the contents of the paragraph. They explain, show, or tell what will follow. These are not specific details. They do not try to convince you by giving facts or examples. Rather, they provide an overview of the contents of the paragraph.

While the topic sentence can be placed anywhere in a paragraph, it is most often placed first in paragraphs in informational articles. Authors do this to make their writing clear and easy to follow. Occasionally a writer will place a topic sentence in the middle of a paragraph to achieve balance. Writers can even put topic sentences at the end of a paragraph to create suspense and mystery. These techniques are most common in fiction and almost unknown in newspaper, magazine, and journal articles, where the goal is clarity and packing the most punch for the word.

To prove their point, authors support their topic sentences with specific details, facts, and examples. The more specific the details, the more readily an audience will be persuaded. Instead of reading all the details slowly, look for nouns and verbs that give you the main idea of each detail. This will give you the information you need without slowing your reading pace.

We've underlined the topic sentences in the following article to show you what we mean. Read through the article to familiarize yourself with topic sentences. At the same time, see if you can find the key nouns and verbs.

Working Safely with Video Display Terminals

The applications of computer technology and the accompanying use of VDTs are revolutionizing the workplaces of America, and their use will continue to grow in the future. For example, according to some reports, there were only 675,000 VDTs in use in U.S. offices in 1976; a decade later, there were an estimated 28 million. The number of VDTs in use in growing rapidly, and in the 21st century there may be anywhere from 40 to 80 million VDTs in the workplace.

In the wake of the expanding use of VDTs, concerns have been expressed about their potential health effects. Complaints include excessive fatigue, eyestrain and eye irritation, blurred vision, headaches, stress, and neck, back, arm, and other muscle pain. Other concerns include general physical discomfort, cumulative trauma disorders, and potential exposure to electromagnetic fields. Research has shown that these symptoms can result from problems with the equipment, workstations, office environment, or job design, or from a combination of these.

Visual problems such as eyestrain and irritation are among the complaints most frequently reported by VDT operators. These visual symptoms can result from improper lighting, glare from the screen, poor positioning of the screen, or copy material that is difficult to read. These problems usually can be corrected by adjusting the physical and environmental setting where the VDT users work. For example, workstations and lighting can and should be arranged to avoid direct and reflected glare, anywhere in the field of sight, from the display screen or surrounding surfaces. VDT operators can reduce eyestrain by taking vision breaks, which may include exercises to relax eye muscles after each hour or so of operating a VDT. The National Institute for Occupational Safety and Health (NIOSH) recommends a 15-minute break after 2 hours of continuous VDT work for operators under moderate visual demands, and a 15-minute rest break after 1 hour of continuous VDT work where there is a high visual demand or repetitive work tasks. Changing focus is another way to give muscles a chance to relax. The employee needs only to glance across the room or out the window from time to time and look at an object at least 20 feet away. Other eye exercises may include rolling or blinking the eyes, or closing them tightly for a few seconds.

Work performed at VDTs may require sitting still for considerable time and usually involves small, frequent movements of the eye, head, arms, and fingers. Retaining a fixed posture over long periods of time requires a significant static holding force, which causes fatigue. <u>Proper work station design is very important in eliminating these types of problems.</u> Some variables of workstation design include the VDT table, chair, and document holder. An individual workstation should provide the operator with a comfortable sitting position sufficiently flexible to reach, use, and observe the display screen, keyboard, and document. Some general considerations to minimize fatigue include posture support (back, arms, legs, and feet) and adjustable display screens and keyboards. VDT tables or desks should be vertically adjustable to allow the operator to move the screen and keyboard. Proper chair height and support for the lower back are critical factors in reducing fatigue and related musculoskeletal complaints. Document holders also allow the operator to position and view material without straining the eyes or neck, shoulder, and back muscles.

The type of task performed at the VDT may influence the development of fatigue. In designing a workstation, the types of tasks involved should be considered when determining the placement of the display screen and keyboard. VDT operators are also subject to a potential risk of developing various musculoskeletal and nerve disorders such as cumulative trauma, or repetitive motion, disorders.

Carpal tunnel syndrome (CTS) is one of the most commonly recognized cumulative trauma disorders among VDT operators. CTS is caused by repetitive wrist–hand movement and exertion. CTS is the compression and entrapment of the median nerve where it passes through the wrist to the hand—in the carpal tunnel. When irritated, the tendons and their sheaths housed inside the narrow carpal tunnel swell and press tightly against the nearby median nerve. The pressure causes tingling, numbness, or severe pain in the wrist and hand. CTS usually can be reduced by stopping or limiting the activity that aggravates the tendons and median nerve, by maintaining proper posture, or, as a last resort, by surgery. For correct posture, VDT operators should sit in an upright position at the keyboard, with arms parallel to the floor. The wrists and forearms may require support, depending on the tasks involved.

Another issue of concern for the VDT operator is whether the emission of radiation poses a health risk. Some workers, including pregnant women, are concerned that their health could be affected by electromagnetic fields emitted from the VDTs. The threat from X-ray exposures is largely discounted because of the very low emission levels. The radio frequency and extremely low-frequency electromagnetic fields are still an issue despite the low emission levels. To date, however, there is no conclusive evidence that the low levels of radiation emitted from the VDTs pose a health risk to VDT operators. Some workplace designs, however, have incorporated changes—such as increasing the distance between the operator and the terminal and between workstations—to reduce potential exposures to electromagnetic fields.

Exercise

Now apply what you learned about topic sentences. Read each of the following paragraphs as quickly as you can, using your hand as a guide to increase your speed. Then underline the topic sentence in each paragraph:

1. Within the next few years, many of us will plug into the morning newspaper. By virtue of powerful communication technology and nifty artificial intelligence techniques, we will be able to gaze into a single viewing device that will offer text, photographs, animation, and film clips. The news will be your news, about your business, your teams. Your morning electronic mail— for what is mail but personalized news?—will come across the same screen.

2. Many in-flight medical problems occur when the plane's environment exacerbates preexisting health disorders. The very dry cabin air aggravates chronic pulmonary diseases and causes dehydration to occur more quickly, so keep yourself hydrated by drinking a lot of water and going light on alcohol. The rule of thumb is no more than two alcoholic drinks and least as many nonalcoholic drinks. Move around the cabin every so often, especially on long flights, to keep your circulatory system functioning.

3. Pressure usually falls rapidly with the approach of a thunderstorm, then rises sharply with the onset of the first gust and arrival of the cold downdraft. It falls back to normal as the storm moves on. This cycle of pressure changes may occur in as little as 15 minutes. If the altimeter setting is not corrected, the indicated altitude may be in error by over 100 feet.

4. In an area poor in almost all natural resources, trees are a primary means of subsistence. They are used as construction materials for homes and for stockades. The leaves are a source of food for animals in the dry season, and the nuts and fruits are a staple of the human diet. Perhaps most important, however, is the fact that the trees are used for fuel. Wood and dung are the primary energy sources for heating and cooking in 90 percent of rural Sahel homes.

5. The journey against avalanches, ice, wind and death began in 1972, at 23,000 feet above sea level in the Afghanistan mountain range. Arlene Blum, an American climber going up a mountain, met a Polish climber who had reached the peak and was descending. Happy at having climbed the 7,000 meters to the top, she said that it was now time for women to climb an 8,000-meter peak.

6. "Retailing on wheels" is a new marketing concept stimulated by the rising price of energy and the need to reduce costs in marketing. The new approach links stores on wheels—large trailers that unfold into small stores—with central, circular malls. The stores-on-wheels drive to the malls, unfold, and hook up like the spokes of a wheel to a central core structure. The mobile stores would most likely be accordioned into smaller stores, complete with shelves,

displays, and checkout counters. The stores could set up in a matter of hours. The central core could be made of canvas, plastic, or any other material, and might have the shape of a dome or tent. A single developer might have a half-dozen or more mobile malls across the country. In addition, units could be leased to retailers. The stores could be driven from site to site, depending on the season, consumer preference, population, and even tourist trade.

7. By and large, businesses can make profits only by producing goods and services that people want to buy— autos, houses, dry cleaning, air travel, cat food. If there is no consumer who is willing and able to buy, the businessperson is out of luck. Maybe the government will temporarily come to his or her rescue with a subsidy, or maybe the businessperson can keep going by using invested capital. But over the long pull, it is customers who are willing and able to buy who direct production in a private-enterprise economy.

8. Since consumer demand largely directs production in a private-enterprise system, it is important to define "demand" accurately at the outset. "Demand" is the schedule of amounts of any product that buyers will purchase at different prices during the stated time period. This definition takes some explaining, since it obviously isn't quite what the word means in daily conversation.

Answers

1. Within the next few years, many of us will plug into the morning newspaper.
2. Many in-flight medical problems occur when the plane's environment exacerbates preexisting health disorders.

3. Pressure usually falls rapidly with the approach of a thunderstorm, then rises sharply with the onset of the first gust and arrival of the cold downdraft.

4. In an area poor in almost all natural resources, trees are a primary means of subsistence.

5. The journey against avalanches, ice, wind, and death began in 1972, at 23,000 feet above sea level in the Afghanistan mountain range.

6. "Retailing on wheels" is a new marketing concept stimulated by the rising price of energy and the need to reduce costs in marketing.

7. But over the long pull, it is customers who are willing and able to buy who direct production in a private-enterprise economy.

8. "Demand" is the schedule of amounts of any product that buyers will purchase at different prices during the stated time period.

Exercise

As you read the following sample passage, do not pay equal attention to every sentence. Instead, quickly scan the beginning of each paragraph for the topic sentence. Then slow your pace and read that sentence carefully. Make up for the lost time by reading more quickly through the rest of the paragraph. At the same time, be on the lookout for nouns and verbs that provide the details that explain the topic sentence. This will give you the details you need and still let you read more quickly.

Electronic Publishing

Electronic publishing has become an important technology in office automation and publication management. It can be used to improve the appearance and impact of documents while lowering publishing costs. However, the proliferation of publishing systems and potential applications makes it difficult for managers and users to make informed decisions on which systems are best for them.

Electronic publishing encompasses a broad range of technologies, computing services, and areas of expertise. By selecting the appropriate technologies and matching these to the appropriate applications, electronic publishing will improve productivity and reduce costs. The key to selecting the best publishing system begins by understanding your organization's publishing needs and goals as well as how the different pieces of technology fit together in a publishing system.

The purpose of this report is to inform users and managers of the technical and management choices and implications associated with selecting and using publishing systems. The report defines electronic publishing, explores the advantages of using electronic publishing, presents selection criteria, and concludes with a discussion of publishing issues.

The nature of this report requires naming vendors and commercial products. The presence or absence of a particular product or vendor does not imply recommendation or endorsement (or rejection) by the National Institute of Standards and Technology, nor does it imply that the products identified are necessarily the best available.

In general, electronic publishing consists of the following processes: (1) creation—including gathering, writing, editing, and illustrating information; (2) composition—including document design, page makeup, typesetting, and pagination; (3) pagination—including printing as well as storage on electronic media such as magnetic tape or CD-ROM; (4) distribution—including handling of printed copies and electronic delivery systems.

Electronic publishing is the use of computer tools to perform these processes and produce documents. The tools

40 are a result of the synthesis of word processing, graphics, electronic typesetting, software, information management, and communications services. The documents, which can range from simple letters or forms to in-depth technical manuals, may contain text, tables, scientific notation, photographs, graphics, and/or line art.

Electronic publishing systems encompass a broad range of technologies from personal computers to mainframe computers, printing systems, scanners, storage devices, and software to integrate these components. Text and graphics
50 can be created on different input devices and output on one or several different types of output devices. Within a single publishing system any or all of these technologies may be used to produce and distribute documents.

Before 1985, publishing was the purview of specialized personnel in publication, graphic arts, prepress, and/or printing organizations. For many, publishing a document meant providing these specialists with a prepared manuscript and then proofing galleys and final pages prior to printing. There was little understanding of or interest in the
60 activities these specialists performed to produce high-quality final products.

However, by 1985 technical advances in the form of workstations with increased computing performance, cheaper storage media, improved graphics displays, and new technology for reproducing images allowed the introduction of desktop publishing (DTP). Capabilities that were once available only on specialized proprietary systems were now available on computing systems found in every office. Virtually every personal computer user could become
70 a publisher. Authors of documents began to take an interest in the different aspects of publishing a document, performing many of the tasks themselves. Moreover, they began to look for methods of streamlining the publishing process, to make it more efficient and effective.

At first, most publishing products were categorized as either desktop publishing or professional publishing products. The distinction between the two categories was based on the number of users or publishers and the type of computer platform. Desktop publishing products were single-user software packages used to develop low-to-medium-quality products such as newsletters, reports, and proposals for laser printer output. Professional publishing products were multiuser products that offered more sophisticated typographic and composition control for the production of large, complex documents such as technical manuals, books, and newspapers.

Today, the distinction between desktop publishing and professional publishing is disappearing as the products become more sophisticated in capabilities and/or available on a wider range of computer platforms. For example, Ventura can be used in a multiuser environment, can handle large, complex documents, and can produce quality typeset documents. Interleaf Publishers, which was once available only on microcomputer network workstations, is available on today's personal computers. In addition, other software applications, such as word-processing packages, have embodied limited publishing capabilities in their newest software releases. These include WordPerfect, Word, and Wordstar. These word processors, sometimes known as word publishers, continue as writing tools but may eliminate the need for separate publishing packages by enabling the author to produce near-typeset-quality final products. These new publishing products, including new versions of old favorites, are a result of increased user sophistication and demand for additional capabilities as well as of continued advances in computing technology.

Since publishing activities may be performed by several people using different vendor systems, it has become

apparent that networking and integrating are essential to the
110 success of publishing. As a result, emphasis is placed on
enabling users to exchange data between different
computers and applications, and to access a variety of input
and output devices.

Reading rate: _____

LESSON THREE: BACKWARD READING

This technique is a little more advanced than many of the others you have learned. As a result, it's not for everyone. Give it your best shot, but don't be discouraged if it doesn't work for you; there are many other techniques that will.

Clearly, reading in both directions is twice as fast as reading in only one. And there's no wasted time. Your eyes do not have to travel back to the start of a line — they're there already. Instead of resting for a second, your hand motion pushes you forward. "But I can't possibly understand a sentence that's written backward," you're probably thinking. Give it a try! Remember that you were taught to read from left to right. People in other cultures read differently. Children in Israel are taught to read from right to left. Children in China are taught to read from the top of the page to the bottom. With practice and patience, you can retrain your eyes — and your brain.

When you read a line of text backward, start by looking for the nouns and verbs. The verbs are the words that describe action. The nouns are words that identify people, places, and things. Nouns that are capitalized are called "proper nouns," and describe specific people, places, and things. If you can pick out these words while reading a line of type backward, this technique will probably work for you. If you can't, just relax.

Try this, instead. As you read forward and backward, mentally summarize each line of type. This way you will not feel forced to understand each individual word, but you will still get the gist of the sentence.

As you read backward, trace your fingers back and forth across the type, like a winding road. To start, place your fingers at the beginning of the sentence. Move your fingers forward, following their motion with your eyes. When you get to the end of the line, make a slight curve and drop your fingers and eyes down a line. Now, using your fingers as a guide, read backward to the left margin. You will find that in one direction it feels like your hand is pushing your eyes across the page. In the other direction, it seems to pull your eyes across the page. Start slowly, reading only a line or two at a time. Don't push speed yet; master the technique first.

Give backward reading a try with this sample passage. Measure your reading speed by recording how many lines you can read in one minute.

Tips for Backward Reading

1. Vary your reading speed by varying how fast you move your hand.

2. Creating small loops with your fingers will help you understand what you have read, but it will slow your speed.

3. Creating bigger loops with your fingers will help you read faster, but you may not grasp as much.

4. If you are having a hard time learning this technique, drop it for a while. You can always come back to it later, after your reading speed has picked up. You may find that you catch on suddenly. Curiously, slower readers rather than faster ones usually find it easier to read backward.

Computers and Brains

"Circuits," "wires," and "computing" may appear to be
strange terms to use for a human organ like the brain, a
mass of flesh and fluid without any electronic parts.
Nevertheless, these are accurate terms because brains and
computers work in very similar ways. Brains think;
computers add and subtract; both use the same basic logic.

All mathematical constructs and human thinking can be
broken down into the same basic steps. Only the highest
10 form of creative activity seems to work on a different
structure, but it may one day turn out that even creative
thinking can be reduced to these steps.

The basic logical steps that support all mathematics and
reasoning are very simple. The most important ones are
AND and OR. AND is a code name for reasoning that says,
"If 'a' is true and 'b' is true, then 'c' is true." This logic is
transferred to electronic signals by means of devices called
"gates." In a computer the gates are made of electronic
parts. In an animal or a person, the gates are nerve cells. No
20 matter what its chemical composition, a gate is an electrical
pathway that opens to allow electricity to pass through when
certain conditions are met. In most cases, two wires go in
one side of the gate, and another wire emerges from the
other side. The two wires represent the ideas "a" and "b."
The single wire on the other side is the conclusion "c."

In a simple computer, the gates are wired together
permanently, so that the computer can do only certain
specific tasks. They can never change their methods, so
they are not intelligent. Larger, more complex computers
30 have greater flexibility. With these computers, the
connections between the gates can be changed, so they can
carry out different tasks. When a computer programmer
wants the computer to complete a different task, he or she

changes the program. The new program takes command of the machine and the new task can be completed. Even though this type of computer has greater flexibility, it is still not intelligent, for it has no inborn flexibility. These qualities—intelligence and flexibility—come from the programmer. A computer with a very large memory can learn
40 from experience, just like an intelligent animal.

A brain that can learn has the beginnings of intelligence. To be intelligent, the brain must have a good memory and wiring inside the brain that allows the circuits connecting the gates to be changed by experiences. In fact, in the most intelligent brains, many circuits are not wired at first. The gates become connected slowly, as the creature learns the next strategies for survival. In humans, the part of the brain filled with blank circuits at birth is greater than in any other animal, giving humans the ability to achieve the greatest intelligence.

Reading rate: _____

LESSON FOUR: USING PRIOR KNOWLEDGE

Authors write to communicate. They make sure that even uninformed readers will be able to understand their point. How do they do this? They build on what their audience already knows, called *prior knowledge.* Since authors have no sure way of ascertaining your prior knowledge, they have to include all the background that you need.

You might think that readers speed up when they encounter prior knowledge, because they recognize something they know. Actually, just the opposite is true! Studies have shown that readers *slow down* when they encounter material they already know. Perhaps it's like meeting old friends on a tour through a strange country. It's a great way to kill an hour while you are on vacation, but it's also a real time-waster. Slowing your reading speed when encountering prior knowledge is a poor reading strategy. And in this age of increasing information, you need a disciplined approach to assimilate new knowledge.

Exercise

First, read through the following passage and underline all the facts you already know. Then reread the passage, skimming over those facts, reading them as quickly as you can. Time both readings and see how much faster you were able to read the second time.

Lucky in Life?

Why do some people seem to get all the breaks? Is it just dumb luck? The fact is, lucky people move through life with a different attitude than most. They prepare for their breaks, and they develop habits that capitalize on good fortune. Whether it is a new career, changing jobs, or just trying to improve yourself, adopting these habits can help your chances of success.

Take calculated risks. Lucky people perform acts that
10 seem daring, but in fact they are playing out informed hunches with a clear sense of success. Don't just sit back in your comfort zone; get out and make the best of new ideas and experiences.

Turn problems into opportunities. Lucky people take second looks at things that other people barely see the first time. If something appears to be difficult, it probably is, but don't let it get the best of you. Think of it as an opportunity to expand your horizons.

Know when to back off. Unlucky people are often stubborn.

20 Out of ego and ignorance, they don't know when to cut their losses and change their course. Lucky people have a knack for getting out "while the getting is good." Never take on things that you can't see an end to. Lucky people are always ready to change course for the right opportunity.

Reach out to people. Lucky people are never too busy to meet new people and to keep up with old acquaintances. For example, they talk with people next to them on an airplane or bus and exchange business cards. They join clubs and other organizations.

30 Spell luck "w-o-r-k." This is one of the hardest lessons to grasp because some people make it look so easy. We see them enjoying their success and have no idea what it takes to get to the top.

The secrets of success are not as mystifying as we may think. They do not exclude happy chances or unfortunate circumstances. They only deny that these things should rule our lives. All it takes is desire fostered by proper attitude.

Reading rate 1: _____

Reading rate 2: _____

Making Prior Knowledge Work for You!

Instead of pausing at prior knowledge, use your time to concentrate on the unfamiliar information. By not wasting your time on facts you already know, you should be able to double or even triple your reading speed! Here's how:

1. Read the topic sentence of each paragraph.
2. Skim the paragraph if the topic sentence indicates that the paragraph contains *familiar* information.

3. Read the paragraph more slowly if the topic sentence indicates that the paragraph contains *unfamiliar* information.

4. As you read, focus on concepts and ideas, not on words.

Exercise

Try this technique on the following passage. Remember to skim those paragraphs that contain familiar information and focus on those that do not. Try to read the familiar information *as fast as you can*. Be sure to keep track of your reading rate with a timer.

Nectar of the Gods

Beer here! Get your ice cold beer here! You probably heard that shouted the last time you were at the ballpark. It seems that beer has become the nation's drink of choice. Whether people are at a ball game, a party, a barbecue, or just getting together with friends, beer is the pick.

It's more than appearance. People throughout the world consume about 22 billion gallons of beer annually. In the United States alone, people drink 24 gallons of beer per
10 person a year. Out of all these beer guzzlers, how many of them know how their brewski is made?

The chief ingredients of beer are barley malt and other cereal grains, water, hops, and yeast. All brewers use the same brewing process. The differences in the flavors of the various beers available are achieved by varying the amount of each ingredient, the length of the brewing process, and the temperatures. The basic brewing process consists of four major steps.

The first step is mashing, mixing the ground malt with
20 water. Also during this step, the brewer adds cereals, such

as corn or rice, to create a mixture called "wort." The brewer then heats the wort to about 150 degrees, stirring it constantly. The wort is then allowed to settle, and the solids sink to the bottom.

Next comes boiling and hopping. During this step, the hops, the dried flowers of the hop vine, are added to the wort. The hops prevent spoiling and give the beverage flavor. The brewer uses about three-fourths of a pound of hops for each thirty-one gallons of wort. The mixture is
30 boiled for two to three hours.

Fermenting is the next step. Here, the brewer adds yeast to cause the formation of alcohol and carbon dioxide. About a pound of yeast is added to each 30 gallons of wort. The temperature is kept at a constant 38 degrees Fahrenheit. It takes a week or two for the beer to ferment.

The final stage is called "finishing." In this step, the brewer compresses and stores carbon dioxide from the wort. The beer then continues to settle and clear. The aging process, in metal vats, takes from three to six weeks. Then the beer is
40 carbonated. Most breweries, especially the large ones, have equipment to collect the carbon dioxide and to carbonate. The beer is then passed through a pressure filter and packaged.

So the next time you have a beer, think about what went into its production. It's more than just going to the refrigerator to grab a can!

Reading rate: _____

LESSON FIVE: FINDING NOUNS AND VERBS

You just learned that reading *unfamiliar* information quickly — and skimming over *familiar* information — can shave significant time off your reading speed. Here's another way to speed up your reading: by focusing on nouns and verbs.

To read faster and to get more from your reading, it's not enough to read unfamiliar information. You also have to concentrate on squeezing key information from the passage. When you read for information, you want to know the answers to these five questions:

- Who?
- What?
- When?
- Where?
- Why?

Reading nouns and verbs can help you grasp the essential meaning of a passage—*fast!* This is because you are not wasting time on unimportant details. Afraid of missing key facts? Your brain will learn to fill in the information that it needs to construct meaning. To see what we mean, read the following sentence. The nouns and verbs are underlined.

When <u>memory chips become</u> even cheaper, you will be able to <u>put</u> more <u>memory</u> into your <u>computer</u>.

When the nouns and verbs are isolated, this sentence becomes:

<u>memory chips become cheaper you put memory computer</u>

We fudged a little, by adding an adjective "memory" to the noun "chips." You can do the same as you read, using whatever key words best help you derive meaning. Start with the nouns and verbs. By concentrating on these words, your brain will best be able to piece together sentence meaning. This technique works especially well at high reading speeds.

To help you master this skill, underline the key nouns and verbs in each of the following sentences. You can also add key words besides nouns and verbs to assist you.

Exercise

1. Software utilities are available to find and repair many problems, but backing up your work on disk is the only guarantee that you will ever see your data again if a system failure occurs.
2. The study revealed that the damage caused by computer viruses in America was $1.08 billion in 1991 alone.
3. Several American companies are working on a permanent cure for computer viruses — to make the hardware virusproof.
4. Micromechanics, the use of tiny machines such as sensors and actuators for work in industry and medicine, is expected to increase dramatically in the next ten years.
5. Every year, thousands of dolphins stray into fishermen's drift nets, become entangled, and drown.
6. Sales of energy-saving compact fluorescent light bulbs are booming in the United States.
7. Insist that the person who uses the computer back up the data at least weekly.
8. Be sure that the disks are stored properly in a safe place.
9. The former Soviet republics need as much help in medical care as they can get from the West.
10. The aquaculture system certainly has an application in small communities or industrial installations.

Answers (Suggested)

1. Software utilities find repair problems backing up work disk guarantee you see data system failure
2. study revealed damage caused computer viruses American $1.08 billion 1991

3. companies working cure computer viruses make hardware virusproof
4. Micromechanics use tiny machines sensors actuators work industry medicine expected to increase ten years
5. dolphins stray nets entangled drown
6. Sales fluorescent light bulbs booming United States
7. Insist person uses computer back up data weekly
8. disks stored safe place
9. Soviet republics need help medical care
10. aquaculture application communities industrial installations

---

LESSON SIX: CLOZE TECHNIQUES

This speed-reading technique is so successful that there is even a type of reading test that concentrates solely on it, the *cloze* test. In a cloze test, key words are omitted from a reading passage. Readers have to select the best words from a list. They find the answers by looking at the *context,* the surrounding text. A cloze test shows how your brain creates meaning when reading at high speed. Fere's an example:

> Sojourner Truth was a brave woman. In the 1840's, if you were an African-American and a woman, and you wanted to stay out of trouble, you kept your mouth shut. But Sojourner Truth told everyone who would _____ about freeing the slaves.

Your mind filled in the missing word—*listen.* Understanding how the cloze technique works can save you enormous reading time and help prepare you for the 21st century information explosion.

Exercise

Complete the following cloze exercises to help you use this method to increase your reading speed. Select the word that you think best completes each of the following sentences.

1. If no means were provided for adjusting altimeters to nonstandard pressure, flight could be _____. (enjoyable, hazardous)

2. Many in-flight medical problems occur when the plane's environment _____ preexisting health disorders. (improves, exacerbates)

3. All technologies require learning: driving a car, for example, is not an _____ act. (intuitive, learned)

4. Users need to be able to accommodate a design to their _____ requirements. (common, specialized)

5. Computer design would improve if engineers and programmers _____ how their wares were being used after the designs left the lab. (observed, ignored)

6. Further, the corporate commitment has begun to _____ to activism in systemic reform. (expand, contract)

7. The employee must have _____ work space to perform each of the tasks required by the job. (small, adequate)

8. Besides being the center of the federal government, Washington, D.C., is a city of _____. (space, museums)

9. A new study by the National Academy of Sciences found that some foods were likely to increase a person's chance of falling victim to cancer, while other foods were likely to _____ the disease. (cause, prevent)

10. There have been many exciting and controversial World

Series, but the most _____ was certainly the World Series of 1919, also known as the Black Sox scandal. (prestigious, infamous)

Answers

1. hazardous
2. exacerbates
3. intuitive
4. specialized
5. observed
6. expand
7. adequate
8. museums
9. prevent
10. infamous

Exercise

Now try completing a cloze paragraph. Select the word from the list that best completes each sentence.

Word List

computer systems	interact	pleasure
glove	legitimacy	pioneered
finger	exciting	moon
	helmet	

Virtual Reality

The technology known as "virtual reality" is among the most
(1) _____ developments in decades.
(2) _____ by the National Aeronautics and Space Administration and VLP Research, Inc., virtual reality surrounds the user with a different existence. How is this accomplished? It's done through some amazingly sophisticated (3) _____ controlled by skilled optical engineers. The user puts on a (4) _____

that contains a different graphics screen for each eye. Depending on the system, the user may also don a (5) _____ or an entire body suit fitted with position sensors and crisscrossed with fiber-optic thread that tells the computer how the user is moving.

Thanks to different computer programs, the user can visit "virtual space," strolling across the (6) _____, flying through a canyon, or swimming deep under the ocean, for example. Colorful vistas of geomorphic shapes fill the horizon. With the point of a (7) _____, the user can rearrange objects in space. Two people can even enter the same virtual space and (8) _____ with each other, cloaked in virtual disguises.

Virtual reality is now seeking (9) _____ in practical applications. Its creators envision that it might be used to visualize complex-system monitoring, architecture, and city planning, for example. It might also be used to simulate three-dimensional assembly. Right now, however, its primary application is (10) _____. But fun does not come cheap. An average system costs about $225,000, including the computers that control the input to each eye. A two-person system runs about $430,000.

Systems like virtual reality help companies dissolve resistance to computers, which keeps computers from enjoying the same consumer acceptance as television and radio.

Answers

1. exciting	6. moon
2. pioneered	7. finger
3. computer systems	8. interact
4. helmet	9. legitimacy
5. glove	10. pleasure

Exercise

Read the following passage, using the techniques you learned in this section. Be sure to time your reading rate and record it at the end of the passage.

Peanut Butter and Pressure

Early in the 19th century, the French chef Nicolas Appert developed a method of hermetically sealing cooked food so that it could be stored for long periods without spoiling. Canning was created, and with it a true revolution in human nutrition. Today, the revolution continues, as a dramatic new development in Japan shows. The new cooking technique preserves food by subjecting it to very high pressure.

The principle behind preserving foods under pressure has
10 been known since World War II, but the technology to make it work was developed only recently, when scientists created equipment able to generate pressures equivalent to 164,000 feet under the ocean.

Here's how the process works for making fruit preserves. Fruit is chopped into very small pieces, sugar is added, and the mixture is sealed in a plastic bag. The bag is then pressurized to 4,000 to 5,000 atmospheres for 10 to 15 minutes. This places the bag under more than five tons of pressure, enough to destroy the cell membranes in the fruit.
20 The protoplasm flows out of the cells and combines with the sugar to create jam. The extremely high pressure kills any bacteria in the mixture, which means that it can be stored without refrigeration for a relatively long period of time.

Japan's Meidi-Ya Company has been making jams, jellies, and fruit sauces since 1991 using this method. The Pokka Corporation uses the same method to produce grapefruit juice. Recently, Mitsubishi Heavy Industries

developed a better pressurizing machine to meet the rising
demand for this process.

Reading rate: _____

5

The Super Six: Reading Methods for the Information Age

LESSON ONE: SKIMMING

Technical material is often so clearly organized that it may appear easier to read than other books, magazines, and newspapers. Nonetheless, comprehension of technical reading material can be low — less than 50 percent — upon first reading, even if you bring a wealth of prior knowledge to the material. The reason for this is that the vocabulary and density of the text are more complex than in other reading. Here's an easy, effective way to increase your speed and comprehension of technical literature, crucial to the 21st century information explosion. Best of all, this method works well on all sorts of texts!

Most people read to find some specific fact of information. They do not want the whole article; just selected portions. One of the best ways to do this is through *skimming*.

How do you *skim* a text? If you do not know where to find

the information in the text, run your eyes down the middle of the page — without reading. Focus on finding the fact that you need. Amazingly, the information will jump right out!

If you cannot find the information, run your eyes diagonally across the page, from the upper-left-hand corner to the lower-right-hand corner. Then skim from the upper-right-hand corner to the lower-left-hand corner.

With practice, you should spend about five seconds skimming each page.

Exercise

Skim the following article to find the answers to these questions:

1. What is the optimum temperature range for a computer?

   _____

2. Why shouldn't you use extension cords on your computer?

   _____

3. How long should you let your computer warm up in the

   morning? _____

4. Is it good to turn your computer on and off several times

   during the day? _____

5. What are your computer's worst enemies? _____

   _____

Computer Maintenance

Computers are such marvelous tools that we often wonder how we ever did without them . . . but sometimes they do seem to have a mind of their own. Certainly they are somewhat temperamental, reacting to even the most minor mistreatment. You can avoid some annoying misadventures and prolong your computer's life if you follow some simple rules.

First of all, don't place your computer near a window. The
10 system should never be exposed to direct sunlight or to variations in temperature. The temperature should be as constant as possible, never falling below 50° Fahrenheit on one end of the scale or going above 90° Fahrenheit on the other. Temperature variations cause expansion and contraction, which in turn cause the chips to back out of their holder. If the temperature variations are extreme, the signal traces on the circuit board can crack and the soldered joints can break. Temperature fluctuations are also harmful to hard disk drives, and affect speed and other functions.

20 In addition, the electrical power must be grounded. The computer should be kept away from radios. Do not use extension cords; they increase circuit resistance. If you must use an extension cord, use a heavy-duty one.

Always let your computer warm up before you begin to work in the morning. Allow at least 15 minutes, unless the building has been very hot overnight. Keep the motor on until you have finished all your work for the day. It is not good to turn your computer on and off several times during the day.

If you do leave the computer on for a long period at a
30 time, be sure to use the screen saver. This will prevent image burn on the monitor screen. If you do not have a screen saver, turn the brightness and contrast levels all the way down when you are not using the computer. Or you can just turn the monitor off.

Your computer's worst enemies are dust and dirt. To keep your computer working well, keep the computer and work area as clean as possible. Another serious cause of trouble is static electricity. You will see its problems most

often in the winter, when the humidity is low. To help reduce
40 the risk from static electricity, be sure the system is properly
grounded, and treat the carpet with antistatic material.

Treat your computer with care and common sense, and
you will avoid expensive and time-consuming repairs. You'll
also avoid the hassle that comes with computer breakdowns.

Reading rate: _____

Answers

1. The temperature should be between 50° Fahrenheit and
   90° Fahrenheit.
2. They increase circuit resistance.
3. Allow at least 15 minutes.
4. No.
5. Dust and dirt.

LESSON TWO: 1, 2, 3—SKIMMING PLUS

Once you have skimmed the text, it's time to build on what you
found out. We call this method *1, 2, 3*. Here are the basic
stages:

1 — Skim the text
2 — Read the text at your fastest rate. Highlight difficult or
     confusing passages.
3 — Reread only the highlighted passages.

Since you have already learned about skimming a text, let's
move directly to stage 2.

Stage 2

After you skim the text, read it at your fastest comprehension rate. As you read the text, place a check mark in the margin of any confusing passages. You might also want to mark places that you have to memorize. But don't slow your reading!

The number of highlighted passages will vary depending on the text and your reading purpose. You will probably have many more marked passages in a technical paper you're reading for work than in a novel you're reading for pleasure. Don't worry about the number of marked passages, but try to mark only the really important or confusing ones.

Use a pencil to highlight your text; hold it as you would hold your finger to guide your eye. This helps you keep up your reading speed while marking text.

Some people have developed specific codes to mark text. A question mark, for example, might mean "confusing text"; a check mark, "memorize." Use these symbols, or develop your own.

Stage 3

Now go back to the highlighted areas and reread them carefully. Take the time to analyze these passages in depth, or memorize them if required. You will find that this will not take as long as you would have imagined, because this will be the third time that you have looked at the same passages.

Exercise

Read the following text by using the 1, 2, 3 method. First skim the text as fast as you can. Then read at your fastest comprehension rate, marking any confusing passages. Finally, read the marked passages carefully and analyze the information they contain. Keep track of your time and calculate your reading rate at the end.

Space Transportation and Industrial Services

Increasingly, private companies are becoming the providers of space transportation and other services that a few years ago were available only from the government. Companies that once built rockets under contract to NASA and the Air Force are now developing private launch vehicles and offering commercial services to satellite owners. New entrepreneurial firms are joining them, seeking untapped niches in the worldwide demand for access to space.

10   The demand for transportation services to launch commercial communications satellites has sparked fierce competition. Even before the space shuttle *Challenger* accident, NASA's shuttle was under a strong challenge from Europe's unmanned *Ariane* booster. The Soviet Union and China are both marketing their launch vehicles to Western users.

    Today, as a result of the post-*Challenger* policy decisions, the space shuttle no longer competes for communications satellite payloads that can be flown on automated rockets.

20 NASA and other federal agencies are actively promoting and supporting the establishment of a U.S. expendable launch vehicle industry.

    While the *Ariane* has captured a major market share of commercial satellites waiting in line for launch opportunities, the U.S. firms McDonnell Douglas, General Dynamics, and Martin Marietta are showing gains through new contract signings. Contracts with these American companies to launch satellites for foreign and international organizations at present amount to approximately $600 million. NASA and

30 other U.S. government agencies are also providing business

to the domestic launch industry through contracts for commercial launch services.

Aggressive marketing of launch services by Russia and China poses an additional challenge, and the overall issue of free and fair trade is a major concern to U.S. launch service providers.

Beyond commercial launch services, some companies have privately developed and marketed upper stages—the small rockets that transport satellites from temporary low orbit to their permanent orbital stations. McDonnell Douglas developed the payload assist module (PAM), and Orbital Sciences Corporation developed the transfer orbit stage (TOS).

Another commercial entry into industrial support services is Astrotech Space Operations Limited Partnership, which has established a private processing facility near Kennedy Space Center for the prelaunch preparations of satellites and other payloads.

In addition, industrial research into the practical uses of the space environment, and anticipated commercial operations emerging from the discovery of economically viable applications, are prompting the development of privately financed and developed space facilities.

Washington-based SPACEHAB, Inc., for example, is privately developing modules that will expand the capabilities of the U.S. space shuttle by increasing the amount of pressurized volume available for orbital research and commercial activities.

Under an agreement with NASA, SPACEHAB will fly its modules aboard the shuttle within the next few years. SPACEHAB will commercially market space in the module and reimburse NASA for standard launch service costs after each mission.

Other concepts for commercially developed orbital

facilities include the industrial space facility (ISF), a free-flying orbiting facility that could house both research and commercial processing activities, and the possible use of discarded external tanks.

70 Increased commercial participation in the provision of space infrastructure and services is being encouraged by the government to expand the range of capabilities to both government and commercial users.

Commercial providers have been invited by NASA to explore potential contributions to the facilities and services that will comprise the space station *Freedom*—the multipurpose, international complex of orbiting modules and support systems scheduled to be placed in orbit in the 1990s.

Reading Rate: _____

LESSON THREE: THE SQ3R METHOD

You can use the SQ3R method for all kinds of texts, but it works especially well with technical reading. What does *SQ3R* mean?

S	Survey
Q	Question
R	Read
R	Recite
R	Review

Here's what you do.

Survey and Question

Before you actually begin to read, preview the text. For books, look at the front and back covers and also the jacket flaps on hard-cover editions. Then glance through the table of contents, introduction, dedication, and author biography. Look to see if there is a glossary or an index.

For technical articles, see if there is an abstract in the front. Glance through it before you begin to read the text. Then check the end of the article for a "Works Cited" page or bibliography. Is there a glossary, a list of difficult terms?

Previewing text can help you better understand its content and meaning. Here are some things to look for and questions to ask. These questions are appropriate for technical reading.

- Who is the publisher? Have you heard of this publisher before? Is the publisher reputable? If the publisher is not well known or if the book has been self-published by the author, you may want to read the material with a more skeptical eye.
- Who is the author? What do you know about this person? Where does the author work? What degrees does the author have? Is he or she a leader or recognized authority in the field?
- How credible is the author's objectivity? For example, how would you feel about a study that claims cigarette smoking is harmless? You might feel one way if the study was written by scientists at the American Cancer Society. You might feel quite another way if it was written by a person working for the tobacco lobby.
- How recent is the material? If you are reading an article about a brand-new technical innovation such as virtual reality or hypertext, you want to get the latest material possible. Keep in mind that it takes about a year for a

book to be published — and that's not counting the time it took to get written! Therefore, even a book with this year's copyright is at least a year old.

Read

When you have completed your survey, read through the text. Read as quickly as you can, but don't sacrifice comprehension. As you read, continue to ask yourself questions about the text. Keep your predictions in mind and change them if necessary. Spend more time on important material, less on details.

Don't worry if at first you have trouble distinguishing important from unimportant details. The more you use the SQ3R method, the easier it will be for you to separate the wheat from the chaff. You may also mark unfamiliar vocabulary as you read and come back later to look up any terms that are key to comprehension. This technique is especially important in technical reading.

Recite

At the end of every paragraph, look up for a moment and mentally summarize the important points you have just read. Think about what you read. Focus on the key details. Then put important material in your own words. This will help you lock in ideas and greatly improve comprehension. You may wish to "recite" to yourself, without saying the words. If it is easier for you, verbalize what you have read aloud. Many times, talking to ourselves can help us recall important information. If you do not force yourself to recite what you have read, you will lose valuable details.

If you cannot recall what you have read, go back over the previous paragraph. Don't spend too much time, but don't let confusion snowball. It's better to take a few seconds to reread now rather than lose the entire meaning of the text. Try it again with this page. Look up and quickly think about what you have read. Then try to summarize what you have just read in a sentence or two. You can do it in your head or write it down. If you are confused, look back over the page for clarification.

As you get more proficient, you will be able to stretch the amount you read before you recite. Many proficient readers look up after every page or two, for example, rather than after every paragraph.

Review

After you have finished the text, look back over the material. Don't waste precious time rereading the entire text. Instead, focus on key points—the title, major headings, key details. Take a second now and look back over the major headings we've included in this section. You'll see how they guide you to key points: Survey and Question, Read, Recite, and Review. At a glance, you should be able to pick out the most important discussion points.

You may mark crucial passages with a pencil or yellow highlighter. This can slow your speed but vastly improve your comprehension. Most speed readers use this technique only with very technical or important documents.

Exercise

Try the SQ3R method with the following passage. Don't forget to time yourself as you read to maximize your reading speed. At the same time, use SQ3R to gain the most comprehension.

Materials Research and Processing

Still in its infancy, the commercial use of space for materials research and processing is a field of interest to industrial scientists and engineers worldwide.

In-Space Experiments

In the extraordinary environment of space, experiments are being conducted that will lay the foundation for future space-based production of high-value goods. Aboard orbiting laboratories, objects float in a weightless state as the familiar influence of gravity becomes almost totally absent. In addition, space offers a limitless, nearly perfect vacuum.

To many people on Earth, the most novel aspect of spaceflight may be the sight of astronauts turning effortless somersaults without touching the surfaces of their spacecraft. But scientists interested in the behavior of materials tend to be fascinated with other curiosities of this microgravity environment. What they are learning could change our lives on Earth.

The Possibility of Dramatic Advances

The opportunity to conduct industrial research in an environment where conditions are so different from those on Earth could result in dramatic advances in our knowledge of materials and processes, leading to new methods of production in Earth-based factories. We may also learn that certain space-processed materials may be sufficiently superior to their Earth counterparts to economically justify space manufacturing. And still other, yet-to-be discovered products may be entirely unique to space and unattainable on Earth.

Superior Crystals Grown in Space

Already, aboard the space shuttle and other spacecraft, special processing equipment has been used to demonstrate that crystals of material that serve as key components of electronic and optical devices can be grown larger and more perfect in the microgravity of space. It may

be economically feasible to manufacturer such crystals in
space, leading to improved semiconductor chips that enable
us to build faster computers.

Pharmaceutical Companies Show Interest

40   A number of American firms, working in cooperation with
NASA, plan to test equipment and processes to produce
semiconductor materials in space aboard the shuttles.
Pharmaceutical companies are keenly interested in the
prospects for producing crystals of superior quality in space.
If the space environment does permit the growth of more
perfect protein crystals, the result could be advances in the
development of new lifesaving drugs. McDonnell Douglas,
the aircraft manufacturer, has already demonstrated the
value of space as a pharmaceutical processing site. On
50   seven space shuttle flights, the company flew its
electrophoresis system, which separates biological materials
far more efficiently than is possible on Earth. Work was
progressing toward scaling up the process to commercial in-
space production until the *Challenger* accident grounded
shuttle flights, forcing the company to put its plans on hold.

Early Experiments

Still other possibilities lie in the processing of unique
glasses, new metal alloys, and composites. Over 400
exceptionally strong and light metal alloys have been
60   identified as potential candidates for space manufacturing.
Government-sponsored materials research in microgravity
dates back to the early years of the space program. Early
materials-processing experiments were conducted aboard
sounding rockets and in ground-based drop towers.
America's Skylab orbital workshop provided the first long-
duration opportunities for materials research in space.

Strong Interest Around the World

As in other areas of commercial space use, the interest in materials research and processing by our space-faring trading partners and other nations is strong and growing. The European Space Agency, which financed and built the shuttle-based Spacelab orbital laboratory, has an established microgravity materials-processing program. Active national programs are being conducted by the Federal Republic of Germany, France, and Japan. The Russian states have produced some 2,000 pounds of space-manufactured crystals aboard its orbiting space stations.

Space Product for Sale

The first commercial made-in-space product offered for sale was developed by Lehigh University working in cooperation with NASA. Using the monodisperse latex reactor aboard the space shuttle, perfectly matched spheres of latex were manufactured for use in calibrating precision instruments such as electron microscopes. Small vials, each containing millions of the latex spheres, are available for purchase through the Commerce Department's National Bureau of Standards as a standard reference material.

Outlook for the Future

It's impossible to predict when additional commercial products from space may become available. But an expanding list of companies is actively laying the groundwork by conducting investigations in ground-based laboratories, aboard specially equipped aircraft and sounding rockets that provide brief periods of microgravity, and in space itself.

As the materials-processing science and technology base builds, the long-range outlook appears promising for commercial uses of the unique characteristics of space. Many believe this area of commercial application, though it

still faces many challenges and will require many years of
100 development, can be expected to provide substantial future
contributions to economic growth through the emergence of
new products and services.

Reading Rate: _____

LESSON FOUR: THE PQRST METHOD

In addition to the SQ3R method, reading specialists have
developed other ways for people to quickly assimilate great
chunks of written material. In this lesson, you will learn
another of these super reading secrets: the *PQRST* method. Try
it and see if it suits your reading needs.

The letters *PQRST* stand for

- Preview
- Question
- Read
- Summarize
- Test

Let's examine each step in turn.

Preview

books by skimming the title, author, publisher, date of publication, preface, contents, chapter headings, graphics, glossary,
and index. This will help you become familiar with the contents of the book quickly.

magazine articles by looking at the title, author, headings,
subheadings, and any pictures or illustrations.

newspapers by paying special attention to the headlines.

correspondence by skimming the letterhead and looking for anything in boldface or italics.

technical articles by skimming the title, author, headings, footnotes, subheadings, bibliography, and any graphics. Also pay attention to any material that is indented, numbered, or set off in any way.

Exercise

Preview the following excerpt from a technical article. Then complete the questions that follow.

Electronic Publishing

Document Printing

Once completed, the document is either printed, displayed, or stored electronically for future presentation. In order for the document to be printed, it must be represented electronically in the language of the printer. This language, referred to as page description language (PDL) or printer command language (PCL), is used to describe to the printer how the finished page should look.

Document Languages

The best-known languages include PostScript, Interpress, and HP PCL. These printer languages are device specific. This means the document can be printed only on output devices that understand this particular language.

Possible Problems

Typically, the publishing software will automatically create the document in the printer language that was specified during installation. A problem arises if either

1. the type of output device that will be used is unknown

2. the document will be printed on several different output devices, each with a different PDL or PCL.

Reasons for Problems

These problems may occur when your organization supports several different output devices, uses a service bureau to print its documents, and/or prints on demand. On-demand printing allows the document to be stored and interchanged for presentation (i.e., printing or display) at a later time and/or at other locations. The document printing can be distributed to the various sites that need the document. They, in turn, print only the number of copies and/or sections of the document that are needed. This reduces the need to warehouse thousands of copies of a document and eliminates the problem of being temporarily out of print.

Questions

1. What did you learn from the title? _____

   _____

2. What did you find out from the headings? _____

   _____

   _____

3. What do you think this article will be about?_____

   _____

   _____

Answers (Suggested)

1. This technical article will be about electronic publishing.

2. Topics discussed included document printing, document languages, possible problems, and reasons for problems.
3. The article will be about electronic publishing, with a focus on printing, computer languages, and possible printing dilemmas.

Question

Now move to the next step in the PQRST method: *Question*. After you have skimmed the text, turn the main ideas — the subheads — into questions. This will give you a focus for your reading and will help you concentrate on the most important information in the text. This technique is a real time-saver because if forces you to zero in on the meat of the text.

The four topics in the previous article were document printing, document languages, possible problems, and reasons for problems. Turning these into questions, we get:

- What is document printing?
- What are some document languages?
- What problems might come up in the printing process?
- What are some reasons for these problems?

Read

Now it is time to read the document at your best rate of comprehension. Try to move as quickly as you can through the text. Because of the preview and question steps, you are already familiar with the text. This familiarity will enable you to read much more quickly than you would have imagined.

Exercise

Try what you have learned so far by previewing, questioning, and reading the following text. Be sure to time yourself so you can keep track of your reading rate.

OSHA Programs and Services

State Programs

The Occupational Safety and Health Act of 1970 encourages states to develop and operate their own safety and health plans. OSHA approves and monitors these plans. There are currently 25 state plan states: 23 states administer plans covering both private and public (state and local government) employees; Connecticut and New York cover the public sector only.

10 The 25 states and territories with their own OSHA-approved occupational safety and health plans must adopt standards identical to, or at least as effective as, the federal standards. Until a state standard is promulgated, OSHA will provide interim enforcement assistance, as appropriate, in these states.

Consulting Services

Employers who want help in recognizing and correcting safety and health hazards and in improving their safety and health programs can receive assistance from a free
20 consultation service largely funded by OSHA. This service is delivered by state government agencies or universities employing professional staff and consultants.

The consultation service offers advice and help in correcting problems and in maintaining continued effective protection. In addition to helping employers identify and correct specific hazards, consultants provide guidance in establishing or improving an effective safety and health program and offer training and education for the company, the supervisors, and the employees. Such consultation is a
30 cooperative approach to solving safety and health problems in the workplace. As a voluntary activity, it is neither automatic nor expected. It must be requested. This program

is completely separate from OSHA inspection efforts. No citations are issued nor penalties proposed for any safety and health problems found in the workplace. The service is confidential.

Safety and Health Program Management Guidelines

Effective management of worker safety and health protection is a decisive factor in reducing the extent and
40 severity of work-related injuries and illnesses and their related costs. To assist employers and employees in developing effective safety and health programs, OSHA published recommended *Safety and Health Program Management Guidelines.* These voluntary guidelines apply to all places of employment covered by OSHA.

The guidelines identify four general elements that are critical to the development of a successful safety and health management program:

   • Management commitment and employee involvement
50 • Work site analysis
   • Hazard prevention and control
   • Safety and health training.

The guidelines recommend specific actions, under each of these general elements, to achieve an effective safety and health program.

For further information on OSHA programs, contact your nearest OSHA office, state program, or consultation project.

Reading rate: _____

Summarize

You're not finished yet! Now it is time to *summarize* what you have read. To summarize a text, put it into your own words. Keep your summaries brief, no more than a sentence or two. With very long articles, summarize at the end of every page or major subdivision. Find the places where it seems appropriate to break. Then look up for a moment or two and go over what you read.

Exercise

Try your hand! Read the following article on juice extractors. As you read, summarize each main division in a sentence or two. Try to read as quickly as you can.

Bottoms Up?

Juice extractors capable of liquefying everything from apples to zucchini are flying off the store shelves. But with the top-priced model costing nearly $400, this is a purchase that deserves some thought.

Available evidence does not support the dubious health claims made by some manufacturers of juice extractors. There just aren't any significant advantages to drinking your fruits and vegetables, as opposed to eating them whole. On
10 the contrary, whole fruits and vegetables seem to be more healthful than juiced ones. The whole produce has one main advantage over its juiced siblings: fiber. Americans consume too little fiber as it is. To turn a fruit or vegetable into juice, the high-fiber pulp has to be extracted. While a number of juicing machines use the entire fruit or vegetable, as opposed to separating the pulp, the resulting liquid has to be diluted or strained to be palatable. You're right back at the starting line.

Summary #1: _____

_____

Gram for gram, a glass of juice may provide more vitamins than a serving of the same fruit or vegetable. For

20 example, a cup of chopped pineapple has 75 calories and
   24 mg of vitamin C. A cup of unsweetened pineapple juice
   has 140 calories and 27 mg of vitamin C. Similarly, a cup of
   canned tomato juice has 40 calories and 45 mg of vitamin C.
   One whole tomato has 25 calories and 2 mg of vitamin C.

Summary #2: _____

_____

Further, making your own juice can be very costly,
because you need far more produce than you might
imagine. To make two quarts of tomato juice, for example,
you will need about four pounds of tomatoes. To make the
same quantity of apple juice requires six pounds of apples.
30 In addition, juicers are messy. They can be very hard to
   clean as well, since the pulp catches in all sorts of out-of-the-
   way places in the machine.

Summary #3: _____

_____

Juicers do have one significant advantage, however. Few
people actually consume the three to five daily servings of
vegetables and two to four daily servings of fruit
recommended as part of a healthy diet. Juices can give
people the vitamins and minerals they are not getting from
eating whole fruits and vegetables. Since juices are
consumed more quickly, people are more willing to drink
40 them. Further, the unusual combinations of fruits and
   vegetables that people concoct with their juicing machines
   may motivate some consumers to increase their produce
   intake.

Summary #4: _____

_____

> Juicers can also be a lot of fun, because your liquid
> creations are limited only by your imagination. Why not
> create a batch of pineapple–carrot–banana–watermelon
> juice? A nice batch of papaya–pineapple? In a jiffy!

Overall Summary: _____

_____

_____

Answers (Suggested)

Summary 1: Since they remove the fiber from produce,
    juice extractors do not appear to offer significant health
    advantages.

Summary 2: Juice does not offer more vitamins than whole
    fruit.

Summary 3: In addition, making your own juice is very
    costly.

Summary 4: Juicers do give people the chance to consume
    more produce.

Overall summary: Although juicers can be fun to use, they
    are also costly and you are better off consuming the fruit
    and vegetables whole.

Test

The final stage in the PQRST method is testing to ascertain
how much material you have retained. While reading special-

ists allow for either formal or informal testing, approach the following two tests as if you were in a formal setting.

Exercise

Below is a passage on child safety. Read it according to the PQRST method, using your fastest reading speed. Then complete the test at the end of the passage. Write your answers in the spaces provided. Be sure to time yourself so you can calculate your reading rate at the end of the passage.

Safety for Kids

Automobile crashes are the leading cause of death and injury among children and young adults in the United States. Every day at least one child dies and 1,000 are injured while riding in a car. Here are some ways to cut down on these devastating injuries. First, always use seat belts. Research shows that 71 percent of deaths and 66 percent of injuries can be prevented by buckling up—correctly. Tragically, in 76 percent of all cases, children are
10 restrained *incorrectly* in their car seats. Contact 800-745-SAFE for guidelines to using children's car seats correctly. Second, make sure that your child wears a helmet when riding a bicycle or using a skateboard. In some cases this is mandated by law; but fewer than 15 percent of all children wear safety helmets while on a bike or board.

Each year nearly 500 children die from choking or accidental ingestion of toxic substances. In 1991 alone, more than 23,000 children accidentally swallowed vitamins. Thirteen children died. As few as six vitamin tablets can kill a
20 small child. How can you help prevent these deaths? First of all, keep all vitamins, medications, plants, cleaning products, makeup, and so on out of the reach of children. Second,

learn CPR, the Heimlich maneuver, and other lifesaving techniques. Contact your local Red Cross, American Heart Association, fire department, or adult education program for course information.

Fires and burns take the lives of 1,200 children under the age of 14 every year. Ninety percent of all children's fire deaths occur in homes without smoke detectors. Make sure your home has smoke detectors, and check them often to make sure they work. Test the batteries and replace them annually. Teach children how to respond to the smoke detector and to fire itself. Make sure that children know escape routes from the home. Hold family fire drills at least twice a year.

Falls are the leading cause of emergency room visits and hospitalizations of children. Falls result in 200 deaths every year. How can you help prevent some of these tragic accidents? Always use restraining straps when your child is in the stroller or high chair. It is equally important to use straps in grocery shopping carts. In 1991, an estimated 21,000 children under the age of four were treated in emergency rooms for injuries involving shopping carts. Most suffered head injuries after falling out of carts. Also pay special attention to children in walkers. The walkers can tip over, especially near staircases. It is also a good idea to barricade windows by placing furniture against them. Window screens are not an adequate protection. Also, keep all balloons away from children. They can easily be sucked into the windpipe. Balloons cause more fatal choking than any other product. Other common items that children can choke on are grapes, hot dogs, hard candies, cherries, raw carrots, nuts, raisins, and popcorn. Ice cubes are also very dangerous; never give a child an ice cube to play with.

Reading rate: _____

Questions

1. What is the leading cause of death and injury among children and young adults in the United States?

    _____

2. What percentage of deaths can be prevented by using seat belts? _____

3. What percentage of injuries can be prevented by using seat belts? _____

4. What percentage of children are restrained incorrectly in their car seats? _____

5. What percentage of children wear safety helmets while riding their bicycles or skateboards? _____

    _____

6. How many children die each year from accidental ingestion of toxic substances? _____

7. List two ways you can help protect children from poisoning. _____

    _____

    _____

8. How many children die each year in fires? _____

    _____

9. List two ways you can help protect children from home fires. _____

_____

_____

_____

10. List two ways you can help protect children from falls.

_____

_____

_____

11. List four foods children should not have because they can cause choking.

_____

_____

_____

_____

12. Should children play with ice cubes? Why or why not?

_____

_____

Answers

1. Automobile crashes
2. 71 percent
3. 66 percent
4. 76 percent
5. Fewer than 15 percent
6. Nearly 500
7. Keep all vitamins, medications, plants, cleaning products, makeup, and so on out of the reach of children.

    Learn CPR, the Heimlich maneuver, and other lifesaving techniques.
8. About 1,200 children under the age of 14
9. Check smoke detectors, teach children how to respond to the smoke detector and to fire itself. Make sure children know escape routes from the home. Hold family fire drills at least twice a year.
10. Always use restraining straps when your child is in the stroller, high chair, or grocery shopping cart. Pay special attention to children in walkers, and barricade windows.
11. Possible answers include grapes, hot dogs, hard candies, cherries, raw carrots, nuts, raisins, and popcorn.
12. No; they can cause choking.

Exercise

Once again, be sure to preview, question, read, and summarize. Then answer the test questions at the end of the passage. Remember to time yourself to record your progress.

NASA's Commercial Development Program

A Partnership with Industry

    Through a family of cooperative agreements with private ventures, and a policy that encourages and assists individual researchers in using NASA's capabilities, the agency has expanded its partnership with U.S. industry.

    Today, more than half of the 50 largest U.S. industrial corporations have become participants in one or more of NASA's programs to encourage increased commercial
10 involvement in America's civil space program. These include cooperative efforts such as joint endeavor agreements (JEA)—a no-exchange-of-funds arrangement where NASA

sponsors spaceflight opportunities for companies that
commit corporate resources to build and conduct industrial
experiments.

3M is one of several firms that have an active JEAs with
NASA. The company has already flown experiments in
crystal growth and organic thin films aboard the space
shuttle and has applied for a number of patents related to its
20 space research activity.

Other Commercial Partners

Other JEA partners plan to investigate the commercial
potential of processing semiconductor materials in space.
Unocal (Union Oil of California) has initiated discussion with
NASA concerning a possible joint endeavor to support the
private development of remote sensing technology for use in
seeking out energy resources.

Another NASA agreement, the space systems
development agreement (SSDA), is helping companies like
30 Geostar Corporation and SPACEHAB get off the ground by
offering launch services on a deferred payback arrangement.

Commercial Launch Industry

NASA assistance and cooperation have been crucial to
the start-up of the fledgling U.S. commercial launch industry.
This includes NASA agreements to privatize the production
of government-developed launch vehicles, provide access to
government launch and support facilities, and use
commercial launch services.

Microgravity Sneak Previews

40 With NASA's help, a growing number of companies are
taking an initial step into space without leaving the confines
of Earth. Industrial experiments in specially equipped NASA

aircraft and ground facilities can provide "snapshot" insights into microgravity processes and enable commercial investigations of remote sensing.

The KC 135 aircraft, the plane in which the NASA astronauts get a taste of what they will experience in the microgravity of space, affords industrial scientists and engineers opportunities to verify the operation of equipment,
50 and even to produce materials samples in a weightless environment.

Other NASA facilities, like the Microgravity Materials Processing Lab at Lewis Research Center in Cleveland, Ohio, also provide access to ground-based microgravity research.

The Earth Resources Laboratory at NASA's Stennis Space Center, near Bay St. Louis, Mississippi, operates research aircraft that support investigations of commercial remote sensing, such as those being carried out by Unocal.

Reading rate: _____

Test

1. About how many of the 50 largest U.S. industrial corporations participate in one or more of NASA's programs to encourage increased commercial involvement in space programs? _____

   _____

2. What are joint endeavor agreements (JEA)? _____

   _____

   _____

3. List two ways 3M is involved in JEA. _____

_____

_____

4. How is Unocal involved in JEA? _____

_____

_____

5. How is SSDA helping Geostar and SPACEHAB get off the ground?

_____

_____

6. What airplane do scientists use to verify the operation of equipment and make materials samples in a weightless environment?

_____

7. What does the Earth Resources Laboratory investigate?

_____

Answers

1. More than half
2. It is a no-exchange-of-funds arrangement where NASA sponsors spaceflight opportunities for companies that commit corporate resources to build and conduct industrial experiments.
3. It has flown experiments in crystal growth and organic thin films aboard the space shuttle and has applied for a number of patents related to its space research activity.

4. It wants to use remote sensing technology to find energy resources.
5. It is offering launch services on a deferred payback arrangement.
6. The KC 135 aircraft
7. It investigates commercial remote sensing.

Now let's take a look at another super speed-reading method you can use to make your reading easier, faster, and more accurate.

LESSON FIVE: THE PARU METHOD

Like the SQR3 Method, the PARU system is an easy way to remember an important and useful way to speed up reading and comprehension. The letters in PARU stand for

- Preview
- Ask
- Read
- Use

Preview

As you learned previously, the way you preview text depends on its nature. Preview a book, for example, by looking over its title, author, cover, introduction, reviewer's comments, table of contents, chapter headings, graphics, index, and glossary. Preview a magazine article by skimming the title, author, headings, and illustrations. Preview a letter by reading the letterhead and signature; a memo, by scanning the heading and closing.

Exercise

Preview this lesson by following the steps above. See how much information you can gather quickly.

Ask

Always read for a purpose, and keep that purpose in mind as you delve into the text. Remember that reading is basically a process of *discriminating,* selecting the material you need and discarding the rest. As you read anything, remember that you must constantly ask:

- What can I gain from this piece of writing?
- What information will it give me that I need?
- How can I best get that information?

Imagine that you are sent into a store to "find something." Since you don't know what you're searching for, you have no idea what to find. But if you're told to go to a store and buy a pair of white sneakers, size 7, that cost less than $50, you will have a clear purpose in mind. This will make your shopping easier and less time-consuming. In a similar way, having a purpose for reading will make your task much easier. In fact, your ability to learn depends primarily on your ability to ask questions, understand the answers, and relate the relevant new information to what you already know. Reading with a specific idea in mind can help you search more efficiently for the information you need.

Read

After you have previewed a text and set a purpose for your reading, it is time to read that text at your best rate of comprehension. As you read, compare what you already know about the subject with what you find out. Read for meaning and to relate new and prior knowledge.

Exercise

Preview the following selection and set a purpose for reading. As you read, continue to ask yourself questions and fit the new knowledge into what you already know about the subject.

Planters Peanuts

How does Planters shell all those peanuts without breaking
them? This may seem unimportant or trivial, but when you
are talking about cleaning, sizing, and shelling 100,000
pounds of peanuts per hour, it becomes a matter of some
importance—especially if you like peanuts as much as I do.

When the Planters plant in Aulander, North Carolina, gets
the peanuts, the little goobers are very grubby. Peanuts
grow in the ground, and when they are dug out, they often
10 emerge with bits of sticks, clumps of dirt, and other rubbish
attached. This whole load is dumped into a reel machine that
removes the rubbish from the peanuts. Then peanuts go
down a conveyer belt to a louver deck that has two-inch-
square openings through which the peanuts will fall. The large
rubbish is then discarded. At this point, the peanut still has
small particles of dirt and grass attached to it. A second deck
screen with small openings does the opposite task; it allows
the particles to fall through and the peanuts to stay behind.

Now that the peanuts are cleaned, it is time to separate
20 them by size. This is done through a series of screens.
There are different-sized holes that the peanuts fall through.

Next, the peanuts have to be roasted. They are kept in
their shells and ride along a conveyer belt from which the
discolored ones are rejected. They are first sorted by an
electric eye, and then by human hands.

Last but not least, the good peanuts are sent to the
shellers. These are semicircular baskets with different-sized
openings. The largest opening is 30/64 of an inch. There are
beaters that rotate at a rate of 200 times per minute. They
30 have sharp edges that strike the peanuts and push them
through the openings. As they are pushed through, the shells
crack open. A fan blows the shells away from the peanuts.

The peanuts are once again sized by screens. Those that
remain in the shell will go into smaller shelling units to be

removed. There are five acceptable grades; those that are too small are used for peanut oil. The whole process takes barely 30 minutes to complete.

Reading rate: _____

Use

Information is enjoyable to have for its own sake, but it becomes truly important when we can *use* it. This is especially true with the 21st century information explosion. Many people will not be able to afford the luxury of reading for pleasure — they will have to read for information. As you read, think about how the information you are gathering can be applied to your reading purpose. Ask yourself such questions as:

- How does this relate to what I already know on the subject?
- Is this giving me facts that I already know?
- What information is really important for my purpose?

You might find that the article is *not* giving you anything new. In that case, you might not even want to finish reading it. Many people believe they have to read to the end of everything. Not so! If you're reading for pleasure, and the book is no longer fun, discard it and move to another. If you're reading for information and the material doesn't contain what you need, set it aside and try something else. Don't waste your time, unless you have time to spare!

Exercise

Put it all together! Try the PARU method with the following selection. Remember to preview, ask, read, and use what you have learned. Time yourself to help keep up your reading speed.

Fiber Optic Future?

A standard modem sends data over telephone lines at 2,400 bits per second. Telephone lines carry voice signals at the rate of 64,000 bits per second. That may sound like a lot, but consider that fiber-optic cables have been reported to carry as many as 1 trillion bits of information per second! This is even more amazing when you realize that in the past 10 years the rates achieved by optical fibers have increased 100 times. At the same time, the cost of fibers fell from $4 to 45 cents per meter. As a result, AT&T and other carriers in the United States and other countries are laying millions of miles of fiber-optic cables every year. The technology is brilliant, but its application remains murky.

Who Foots the Bill?

Fiber-optic suppliers, users, and regulators have to agree on where the cable is going to go, who will pay to install it, who will own the resulting network, and what services it will supply. Each of those questions also affects the technical aspects of the program: bit rates, switching mechanisms, software protocols, and so forth. Until these issues are resolved, the network cannot be implemented.

Unresolved Problems

There are many problems. The telephone companies, for example, are not used to transporting data. At current capabilities, for instance, it takes almost three hours to transmit a single, soundless TV still by modem. In addition, the computer companies are not used to the idea of universal service. Progress in this area has been slow and disjointed. For example, Internet was a combination of the four-node network begun in 1969. Today it connects nearly 1,000 networks in at least 175,000 computers. It has subscribers in 35 countries. Some liken it to the eighth wonder of the world.

A Public Internet?

A number of people have called for a public version of Internet to link all these technologies. A national information infrastructure would help solve all the difficulties sketched above, but it cannot come about by itself. The Office of Science and Technology Policy, part of the federal
40 government, has thrown its support behind a high-performance computing measure. Under provisions of this proposal, the government would establish a national research and education computer network that would link all university computers to those in government and industry. In the meantime, ITT has codified international standards for the unified voice and data channel, ISDN. Europe and Japan have already established these standards. By 2025, Japan will be connected by a fiber-optic telecommunications system that will run into virtually every home and office. The
50 system would make possible TV phones and customized electronic newspapers. The United States has been slower to move on the initiative. No doubt this is in part because of the staggering cost. Japanese experts estimate the cost for uniting the entire archipelago with a complete network will be between $174 and $208 billion.

Reading rate: _____

LESSON SIX: INSTANT REPLAYS

A good way to strengthen your comprehension skills is to make a quick summary of your reading. It's easy to do. Just look up at the end of each page and summarize what you have read in a few phrases or sentences. To start, you may want to jot down your summaries on a piece of paper. Later, when you feel more comfortable with this technique, you can mentally summarize your reading.

Here's a sample of the technique. Read the following passage. Try to summarize it yourself. Then read the summary we have provided. See how closely yours matches ours.

Sample Passage

Others may ask you how you define success. This is more difficult. Success is relative; not everyone wants to put together a $4 million conglomerate, or become president of the United States, or win the Nobel Peace Prize. It is usually wise to give up such grandiose ambitions, which tend to degenerate into lazy daydreams. The best way to succeed is to begin with a reasonably realistic goal and attain it, rather than aiming at something so far beyond your reach that you are bound to fail. It's also important to make a habit of succeeding; the easiest way to start is to succeed at something, however small, every day, gradually increasing the level of your ambitions and achievements, like an athlete in training.

Summary: People define success in their own way. To become a success, start small. Succeed at something every day.

Exercise

To help you master this technique, we have included a few exercises. Read the following paragraphs. Then jot down a one- or two-sentence summary of each. Don't worry about writing full sentences. Just try to get down your ideas as clearly and succinctly as possible.

1 What Is a Drug?

A common definition of the word "drug" is any substance that in small amounts produces significant changes in body, mind, or both. This definition does not clearly distinguish drugs from some foods. The difference between a drug and a poison is also unclear. All drugs become poisons in high enough doses, and many poisons are useful drugs in low enough doses. Is alcohol a food, a drug, or a poison? The body can burn it like a fuel, just like sugar or starch, but it causes intoxication
10 and can kill in overdose. Many people who drink alcohol crusade against drug abuse, never acknowledging that they themselves are involved with a powerful drug.

Summary: _____

_____

_____

2 Values

If we want auto safety but continue to believe into auto profits, sales, styling, and annual obsolescence, there will be no serious accomplishments. The moment we put safety ahead of these other values, something will happen. If we want better community hospitals but are not willing to reduce the amount we spend for defense, for highways, for household appliances, hospital services will not improve. If we want peace but still believe that countries whose
10 ideologies do not match ours are inevitable enemies, then

we will not have peace. What is confusing is that while we have wanted such things as auto safety, hospital care, and peace, we have tried getting them without changing our value system; that is, while continuing to accept those underlying values that stand in the way of what we want.

Summary:_____

_____

_____

3 Pizza

One widely held misconception concerning pizza should be laid to rest. Although it may be characterized as fast food, pizza is *not* junk food. Especially when it is made with fresh ingredients, pizza fulfills our basic nutritional requirements. The crust provides carbohydrates; from the cheese or meat or fish comes protein; and the tomatoes, herbs, onions, and garlic supply vitamins and minerals.

Summary: _____

_____

_____

4 Not-So-Wild Life

The truth is, deer are a long way from being an endangered species. They survive in a people-dominated environment almost as well as the rat, because people obligingly kill off the deer's predators. In a classic experiment a few years ago in the Kaibab National Forest in Arizona, local hunters prevailed on government rangers to eliminate the entire

cougar population so people would be the only deer
predators. People turned out to be less efficient than the
10 cougars. In a few years the forest was populated with
thousands of bony deer starving to death; all vegetation
within their reach had been gnawed down to the bare wood.
At great expense, the government had to trap cougars and
bring them to the Kaibab National Forest. As a matter of fact,
despite the number of deer killed every year by people and
predators, deer are more abundant in American today than
when Columbus arrived.

Summary: _____

_____

_____

Answers (Suggested)

1. The definition of "drug" is not clear; it does not take into account poison and alcohol, for example.
2. We must change our value system if we want to accomplish what we say we want.
3. Pizza is not junk food.
4. Deer are not endangered; on the contrary, they are far more abundant than people realize.

Now try an instant replay with the following passage. Either summarize each paragraph or the entire passage. But don't let the summary get in the way of your reading speed.

Reading Problems

What prevents people from reading as fast as they can?
There are three main reading faults people need to correct.
    The first is *rereading.* How often have you been reading

when you have stopped and reread the previous few lines?
Poor readers spend as much as one-third of their time
rereading.

The second fault is *vocalizing,* or saying the words aloud
as you read. Readers who don't actually say the words aloud
10 but feel them in the back of their throats are doing the same
thing. In either case, it's really slowing down your reading!
One way to solve this problem is to suck on a piece of hard
candy or chew some gum. That will make you aware of the
problem and help you break it. Another way to help you
improve your concentration is with music. Nonvocal music
works best, so you are not distracted by the singer's voice.
Studies have shown that the privacy of music helps increase
comprehension and cut back sharply on vocalization. The
third fault is *fixations,* stopping too long on single words. In
20 the average paperback book, there are about 300 words per
average page. If you were to fixate on every word, your eye
would stop 300 times per page! Imagine how long it would
take to read one page!

Reading rate: _____

Summary: _____

_____

_____

_____

6

Not All Reading
Is the Same!

Reading is reading, right? Wrong! Not all reading is the same! Vocabulary, sentence structure, word choice, and subject matter are just some of the factors that determine if a text is easier or harder to read.

Amazingly, technical material is often easier to read than a serious literary novel. This is because technical material usually has a logical organization that makes it easier to grasp the information. In addition, readers often come to the text with a lot of background information of their own. They are not entering a totally unfamiliar literary world; rather, they are on familiar technical ground.

Your purpose for reading and your attitude toward your task are also crucial factors in your reading success. The reason *why* you have picked up a specific text can strongly determine how easily you read it.

LESSON ONE: ACTIVE READING FOR THE 21ST CENTURY

Reading a text is not just looking at words. Rather, reading is gathering and sorting information to create meaning. Skillful speed-readers have learned how to condense this process.

We can say that reading a text is like meeting a new person. You don't just sit back and say, "Entertain me." Rather, you take an active role in the conversation, shaping and guiding it to get the information you want or to make the impression you choose. The best readers are those people who take an active role in the text. They interact with it to get the information they need. Here are some quick hints for active reading. Throughout this book, you'll learn more about active reading.

Strategies for Active Reading

1. **Apply what you already know**

   Don't automatically assume that the writer is *the* expert in the field. If you are reading technical material in your area, you might very well be as knowledgeable as the writer. At the very least, you are bringing prior knowledge to the text. Apply that knowledge to what you read.

2. **Interact with the writer**

   Being an active reader is just that—being *active*. Respond to the text. Don't accept what you read uncritically. If you think the writer is full of baloney, say so. Don't just sit back and let the information wash right over you. Agree or disagree, feel happy or sad—respond to the text!

3. **Predict outcomes**

   Keep thinking about what is going to happen in the text. Try to figure out the writer's plan of organization. Ask yourself, "Why is the information I just read important? How will the writer build on these facts later? What does this information mean to me and my life?"

---

4. Try to solve problems

If you read a confusing sentence or lose track of what the author is trying to say, don't just plow ahead. Stop and think about what you read. We're not advising long-term stops here, but make sure you don't lose the thread of what you're reading. Otherwise, like a snowball gathering speed down a hill, you could end up in an avalanche of confusion. Also, use context clues to guess the meaning of unfamiliar words.

5. Summarize

Stop every page to summarize what you have read. Don't go ahead until you clearly understand the text. Make new predictions or revise ones that were not correct.

Reading for Literal Information

Literal information is stated outright in the text. You can point to the place where the information is found. Most often, literal information is facts, dates, names, and mathematical formulas. Here are some examples of literal information:

- In 1979, Elmer Winter started Operation 4000 to train and create jobs for 4,000 young men in his home community of Milwaukee.
- An average of 150 people die and 250 are injured by lightning each year in the United States.
- India is a major endemic country, with more polio cases than any other country in the world — an estimated 45 percent of the world's total.
- Most people feel uncomfortable discussing certain health matters, and for many older men, the condition of their prostate is one of them. Yet reports of prostate cancer continue to increase, with an estimated 132,000 new cases reported in America alone during 1992. This year, 34,000 men in America will die of the disease.

- Each day Earth experiences about 44,000 thunderstorms, producing 8 million flashes of lightning.

Exercise

Many people memorize literal information for quick recall. Read the following passage for literal information. Then see how many literal details you can find. If you own the book, you can underline the details in the text. If you have borrowed the book from someone, write the literal details on a separate sheet of paper.

Revolution—or Reaction?

Like most revolutions, this one has its roots in economics. The romance between computing and communications is both driving and being driven by the burgeoning services sector. Nearly 75 percent of America's workers are employed in services, up from 55 percent in 1948. And those services have, in the words of one communications expert, "a voracious appetite for information technology."

"Services providers now own about 85 percent of the total U.S. stock of information-technology items," says one analyst in the field. Computing and communications equipment is smack in the middle of this revolution. Whereas manufacturing industries spend 10 percent of their capital on information technology, the service sector's allotment has doubled in the past decade to almost 20 percent.

But recent events show that—information economy or not—people are not prepared to swallow information technology whole. Some attempts to weave computer and communications technology into the fabric of daily life have fallen on very hard times. The videotext consumer-information services are a case in point. Knight-Ridder spent $50 million on its Viewtron project before yanking it in 1986.

Scholastic, one of the largest children's publishers in the world, lost millions in its first run with educational software in the 1980s. No one has done well with electronic banking, either: years after its introduction, fewer than 100,000 people nationwide bank by computer.

Answers (Suggested)

1. Nearly 75 percent of America's workers are employed in services, up from 55 percent in 1948.
2. "Services providers now own about 85 percent of the total U.S. stock of information-technology items."
3. Manufacturing industries spend 10 percent of their capital on information technology.
4. The service sector's allotment has doubled in the past decade to almost 20 percent.
5. Knight-Ridder spent $50 million on its Viewtron project before yanking it in 1986.
6. Scholastic lost millions in its first run with educational software in the 1980s.
7. Fewer than 100,000 people nationwide bank by computer.

LESSON TWO: READING MAGAZINES FASTER

You have already learned a number of techniques to help you read technical material more quickly and accurately. Reading magazine articles, however, requires a different approach.

The key to reading a magazine article faster is analyzing its *structure*. This will tell you how the information is arranged, so you can pick out what you need to know. In this section, you will learn how to take an article apart quickly, to get the information you need and want.

The Structure of a Magazine Article

Here's what you can expect to find in a popular magazine article.

1. *The "grabber" or "teaser"*. To get you to read the article, the author begins with an attention-getting device. Unlike the writer of a technical piece, who usually has a built-in audience, a popular magazine writer knows that you do not have to read his or her piece. As a result, the author must tease you to attract your interest. This "grabber" or "teaser" can be an intriguing headline or title, a brief story, a startling statement, or even a provocative illustration or picture. Frequently, magazine authors and editors use more than one of these methods. For example, you might find a catchy snippet of dialogue in the opening and a controversial photograph to hook your interest and reel you in.

2. *The thesis*. Next comes a clear statement of purpose. This explains why you should read the article. It might describe what it can teach you, for example, or zero in on why this selection is of interest to you.

3. *The body*. The "body" is the primary part of the article. It contains the writer's main ideas. To illustrate the point or to convince you of the thesis, the writer will include specific details, facts, examples, illustrations, and pictures. There may also be statistics, comparisons, testimonials by famous people, charts, or other graphic materials.

4. *The "climax."* To sustain interest, the writer will pull together all the ideas in a dramatic ending. It may be tightly restrained or highly emotional, but it is rarely dull! The ending may also call for some type of action on the reader's part, such as writing a letter or making a telephone call.

Be Picky

How can you save time reading a magazine article? Follow these steps:

1. Read the title and author.
2. Read the first two or three paragraphs to get an introduction to the topic.
3. Read the first sentence of each additional paragraph. This will show you how the author develops the thesis.
4. Read the final paragraph to see how the author sums up the thesis.

Using this method, it should take you about *two minutes* to read the average magazine article. If you then want to go back and read the article in depth, you will find that your reading time has been drastically reduced.

But remember that speed-reading is not only reading faster — it's also knowing what to read. If the thesis does not interest you much, you might be better off reading something else. Weigh your time and interests. If you're stuck in line at the ATM machine or the deli, you're much better off reading something of marginal interest than tapping your foot impatiently and glaring at your watch. Remember: *any* reading will increase your speed and comprehension. Even if it's a magazine that normally does not interest you, don't waste the time: read! But if you have a choice of reading materials, pick what will teach you the most or entertain you the best.

Four Structural Organizers

Let's say that the thesis *does* interest you, and you decide to read the article. Then concentrate on the information in the body. Let the structure of the article guide your reading pattern. By recognizing the structure, you will be able to see how the information is arranged. This will tell you where to focus your attention and best spend your time. There are several main ways magazine writers present their material.

- *Order of time.* Here, the writer arranges information as it occurred, from the first event to the last. This arrangement gives the writer a great advantage by allowing him or her to build the facts to a climax at the end. It is not as good an arrangement for the speed-reader, however. Why? Because it can take you longer to read an article where all of the details are given equal weight. You cannot skip over information, because you do not know what facts will prove most important later on.

    How can you use order of time to your advantage? Look for signposts that clue you to main information. Words and phrases to look for include:

first	second	third, etc.
then	next	later
so	when	during
in the future	now	soon

- *Order of space.* With this method, the writer begins at a certain point in space and moves from there. The article can be arranged from country to country, for example, or from state to state. The spatial focus may also be much more narrow. It may be from room to room, or even from one place to another within a room. The writer may begin a piece by focusing on the floor, move to a table, and end up on the ceiling, for instance.

    To find information in articles organized this way, focus on the specific place that interests you. For example, you might be interested in one country, state, or city, rather than all the places profiled in the article.

    Also look for transition words that show location, such as:

over	under	here
there	beside	near

- *Cause and effect.* With this structure, the writer sets up the situation and then describes the results. Often, skillful writers will trace more than one cause and one effect, even within a situation that seems straightforward. Describing the causes of smoking, for example, the writer might include curiosity, a desire to lose weight, and peer pressure. Effects might include social ostracism and economic problems along with the more familiar health risks.

  To make the best use of your time, focus on the specific issues that interest you. Read only those causes and effects that shed new light on the issue, for instance, rather than slogging through the entire argument.

- *Problem solution.* Within these articles, authors will state a problem and offer one or more solutions. Unless the single solution is very strong, the writer will describe several possible responses. Since these are often arranged from least to most effective, direct your eyes toward the end of the article. That's where you are apt to find the most intriguing, most strongly supported information.

  Keep in mind that any of these methods may be combined. Order of space and order of time, for example, often go hand in hand, as one depends on another. As a result, you may have to look for more than one method to guide your reading.

  When two or more methods are used, often one will be dominant. Look for the *signposts,* the key words, that guide the writer's thoughts. Remember to read the *thesis* for the main idea as well.

Practice

Read each of the following passages and identify its structure according to the four organizers just discussed. To help you decide, look for signposts such as transitional words and phrases.

1. Everyone by now is aware that air-conditioning is an energy glutton. It uses nearly 10 percent of all the electricity produced. Such an extravagance merely to provide comfort is strikingly at odds with all the recent rhetoric about national sacrifice in a period of menacing energy shortages. Other modern industrial nations, such as Japan, Germany, and France, have managed to thrive with mere fractions of the artificial coolness used in America. Here, we have become so profligate in its use that the air-conditioner has become a glaring symbol of the national tendency to overindulge in every technical possibility, to use every convenience to such excess that the country looks downright piggish.

   But not everyone is aware that the high cost and easy comfort are merely two of the effects of the vast cooling of America. In fact, air-conditioning has substantially altered the country's character and folkways. With the dog days at hand and the thermometers up, it is a good time to take stock of what air-conditioning has done besides lowering the indoor temperature.

Structure: _____

2. The history of Florida is measured in freezes. Severe ones occurred in 1747, 1766, and 1774. The freeze of February 1835 was probably the worst one in the state's history. But because more growers were affected, the great freeze of 1895 seems to enjoy the same status in Florida that the blizzard of '88 once held in the North. Temperatures on the Ridge on February 8, 1895, went into the teens for most of the night. It is said that some growers, on being told what was happening in the groves, got up from their dinner tables and left the state. In the morning, it was apparent that the Florida citrus industry

had been virtually wiped out. The groves around Keystone City, in Polk county, however, came through the freeze of 1895 without damage. Slightly higher than any place around it and studded with sizable lakes, Keystone City became famous, and people from all over came to marvel at the lush groves in the middle of the wasteland. The citizens of Keystone City changed the name of the town to Frostproof.

Structure: _____

3. It is not considered good for people to snoop into the lives of others in order to help them. This is considered an invasion of privacy, stepping over the carefully drawn line of good manners. Nowhere is this more evident than in a city or suburban neighborhood. I believe that line can be maintained, without awkwardness to anyone, but still afford us the chance to know and help our neighbors. It is possible to be on good sidewalk terms with people who are very different from oneself, and even, as time passes, to be on excellent terms with them. Such relationships can endure for decades. Let me explain how.

Structure: _____

4. October is the richest of seasons: the fields are cut, the granaries are full, the bins are loaded to the brim with fatness, and from the cider press the rich brown oozings of the York Imperials run. The bee bores to the belly of the yellowed grape, the fly gets old and fat and blue, it buzzes loud, crawls slowly, creeps heavily to death on sill and ceiling. The sun goes down in blood and pollen across the bronzed and mown fields of October.

Structure: _____

5. The first period of sleep is always NREM. It consists of four stages, during each of which the sleeper becomes more remote from the sensory environment. Children in particular are virtually unwakable during the fourth stage. Even if they can finally be roused, it may be several minutes before they return to awareness. This deepest fourth stage is the period during which most of the talking in one's sleep, sleepwalking, night terrors, and bed-wetting by children take place. After the fourth stage, the sleeper retraces all the stages back to lighter sleep. The downward progression into the first deep sleep is smooth, but the upward progression is marked by irregular jumps from one stage to the other. The first REM period begins about 70 to 80 minutes after a person has fallen asleep and usually lasts for only about 10 minutes. The entire stage averages about 90 minutes, but with some individuals it is as short as 70 minutes and with others as long as 110.

Structure: _____

6. Then the United States did two things for Japan. It placed an embargo on the sale of oil needed to sustain Japan's armies, and it put all American warships into one handy disposable package in a harbor in Hawaii. A better combination of stick and carrot to drive the Japanese into war would be hard to imagine. The war chiefs saw their opportunity and struck, and Japan was committed to the forlorn, hopeless adventure. The Japanese would take oil from the British in Burma, by force. They did that. Then they would use valor and skill to make the United States agree to their keeping the loot. But this could not be.

Structure: _____

7. Only idealists fail to realize that a mass television system cannot exist without the support of sponsors, that the massive cost of maintaining it as a free service cannot be met without the massive income from selling products. You have only to read of the unending struggle to provide financial support for noncommercial television for further evidence.

Besides, aren't commercials in the public interest? Don't they help you choose what to buy? Yet some say commercials diminish human worth, infuse and harden outmoded social attitudes, create pervasive discontent, and create psychological fragmentation. But don't they provide needed breaks from programming? . . .

What has to happen to mass-media advertisers as a whole, and especially on TV, is a totally new approach to their function not only as sellers but also as social influencers. They have the same obligation as the broadcast medium itself: not only to entertain but also to reflect, not only to reflect but also to enlarge public consciousness and human stature.

This may be a tall order, but it is a vital one at a time when Americans have ceased to know who they are and where they are going, and when all the multiple forces acting upon them are daily diminishing their sense of their own value and purpose in life, when social upheaval and social fragmentation have destroyed old patterns, when survival depends on new ones.

Structure: _____

Answers

1. cause and effect
2. order of time

3. problem solution
4. order of space
5. order of time
6. cause and effect
7. problem solution

LESSON THREE: READING NEWSPAPERS FASTER

Like magazine articles, newspaper pieces follow a set structure. The information in news articles is arranged from *most to least important*. The most important information is at the beginning of the article; the least important, at the end. This is called the "inverted pyramid" style.

All well-written news articles contain the "five w's and h" in the lead paragraph: *who, what, when, where, why, and how*. This enables busy readers to skim only the first two or three paragraphs of each news article to get the "meat" of the piece. It also makes it easier for editors to cut articles when space is tight. They simply lop off the paragraphs at the bottom.

Understanding the structure of a news article can save you a great deal of reading time. Here's the method to use when you read a news article:

1. Read the headlines to select the articles that interest you.
2. Read the first two or three paragraphs to get the "meat" of the story.
3. Read on *only* if you need more details or are unusually interested in the story.

Exercise

Read the following news story according to the method described above. Be sure to time yourself and compute your reading rate at the end.

Wider American Role in Bosnia

Amid questions around the world about America's commitment to the Western alliance and its role in halting aggression in Bosnia-Herzegovina, America today offered to send 300 combat troops to Macedonia to prevent the war in the Balkans from spreading.

10 And in an action that could prove to be more dangerous for American fighting forces, the Secretary of State agreed at last week's NATO meeting that the U.S. would provide air cover for U.N. forces anywhere in the region. This agreement set the stage for America's strongest military actions in the region thus far.

America also agreed to participate in U.N. retaliations against Serbian attacks in the protected zones. It also agreed to break 20 through Serbian blockades of convoys carrying food and medical supplies.

The U.S. has insisted that its air support would protect only the U.N. forces, not the safe areas themselves. In effect, experts predict that there will not be much distinction between the two.

The Secretary of State was repeatedly challenged at today's news conference to defend America's refusal to contribute 30 ground troops to help the 10,000 French, British, Spanish, Canadian, and other troops in the U.N. forces that are trying to protect the Muslims and restore peace in Bosnia.

The NATO announcement welcomed America's involvement. The air forces will be under the command of the U.N.

The U.S. offer to send troops to Macedonia, while refusing to do so in
40 Bosnia, confirmed the distinction America has maintained in this matter. The State Department has maintained that the rescue of Bosnia is of deep humanitarian concern but not of strategic interest to the U.S. Sending troops to Macedonia is in America's strategic interests, to ensure that the conflict does not spread outside the Balkan area.

Reading rate: _____

Critical Reviews

Critical reviews in a newspaper have a structure different from news stories. Many times, reviewers will place their opinion at the *end* of a piece, devoting the initial paragraphs to providing necessary background, establishing the author's credentials, or giving a brief plot summary. As a result, you should read a movie, book, or theater review differently from the way you read a news story.

Here's the method to use when you read a critical review of a book, movie, or play:

1. Read the first paragraph or two to understand the background and plot.
2. Then read the last few paragraphs to get the critic's opinion.
3. If you are very interested in the piece, go back and read the middle paragraphs.

Exercise

Read the following book review according to the method described above. Be sure to time yourself and compute your reading rate at the end.

The New Revolution in Russia

Since the breakup of the Soviet Union three years ago, there has been a continuing fear that an authoritarian, nationalistic regime would gain power among the disparate states. The Russians, faced with the brutal loss of their empire, the complete breakdown of their economy, escalating crime rates, and pressure from minorities, do indeed appear to be more open than ever before to the appeal of a demagogue. As Harriet Sizemore makes abundantly clear in her new
10 book, *Russia Today,* such fears are not unwarranted.

As well as describing broad cultural and historical trends, Sizemore focuses on individuals. She describes well-known émigrés who endorse openly fascist ideas and thus shed light on today's Russian extremists and lunatic fringe. She also describes mainstream right-wing movements within the country that pose a significant threat to democratic reforms and internal unification.

At present, the history of Communist rule in Russia suggests that broad segments of the population are against
20 political movements based on hatred and bigotry. The roots of Russia's extremists may be broad and deep, but they have yet to flourish in post-Soviet Russian soil. It appears that the current government will endure, at least for the immediate present.

Sizemore, a longtime international correspondent for the *Herald,* has written a provocative, insightful, and engrossing book. It's a must read for anyone concerned with the shape of the world in the 21st century.

Reading rate: _____

Quick Reading Hints

1. **Quickly preview the text.** Find these elements:

   • What information can you get from the titles, headings, and subheadings?

   • What is the subject of the text?

   • Who is the intended audience?

   • Are you required to respond to the text by writing a letter or memo, or making a phone call?

2. **Read the article.** Mark places in the text you think are important. Mark confusing places that will need rereading.

3. **Review what you have read.** Make a brief summary in your head. Note any action you might have to take.

LESSON FOUR: READING NONFICTION AND FICTION

Earlier in this chapter, you learned that not all reading is the same. As a result, you know that you can't read a book the same way that you read magazines and newspapers. Fortunately, you *can* apply many of the techniques you have already learned to reading books. In this lesson, we're going to teach you special techniques that will help you read books much faster and more accurately.

Book publishers and authors realize that you are swamped with reading—because they are as well! To help you, they provide easy-to-use reading aids in all their books. Let's look at some of them now.

Book Covers and What They Tell You

Why did you pick *this* book? If you say it's because the subject interested you, why didn't you select another book on speed-reading? You might have selected this book — or any book, for that matter — because of its cover. Perhaps the design attracted you. But as a savvy consumer, you go beyond the surface. The cover can tell you a great deal about a book, and that can save you precious reading time. Here are some elements to consider.

1. *Design.* The design of the book cover goes a long way to suggest its contents and style. Different choices of color, art, and type can either suggest a contemporary, readable tone or a more old-fashioned approach.

2. *Title.* First, the title of the book, especially of a work of nonfiction, tells you what the book is about. This allows you to make a judgment about the content right away. Is this a book that interests you?

3. *Author/Editor.* Have you heard about the author and/or editor before? Have you read any other books by this author? If so, did you enjoy them? Would you recommend them to others? Further, what are the author's credentials to write a book like this?

4. *Publisher.* Evaluate a publisher as you would an author. Have you heard of the publisher? What other books along this line has the publisher produced?

5. *Cost.* Don't ignore the price of a book. More expensive does not always mean better. And, in some instances, less expensive could mean an out-of-date publication. The book should be competitively priced, not too much more or less than similar titles on the same topic.

6. *Publisher's Blurb.* There is usually a block of copy on the front or the back of the book that describes it. Read the blurb to see what issues the book will explore. Does the book offer the information you need?

7. *Summary.* Pay special attention to the summary. It may appear on the back cover or the inside cover flaps. It is especially useful for works of fiction, such as novels, short stories, and plays. The summary should briefly

describe the plot, the characters, the setting, and the conflict. Reading the main events of the plot can help you keep the events in order; reading thumbnail sketches of the characters will help you recall their names, occupations, and primary traits. In addition, knowing the setting ties the action to the place and time. The summary is one of the most important reasons to preview a book because it can help you understand everything that will follow.

These seven steps should take you only a few moments, and they can give you a surprisingly large amount of information.

Prefatory Material

The *prefatory material* is the information that comes before the main text. Read these sections through to find out more about the book and to help you decide if the book is right for you.

1. *Copyright information.* The copyright data will tell you when the book was published. With a novel, this is not especially critical, but it *does* matter with a nonfiction book, especially one on technology, media, or other timely subjects. In these instances, you are going to want to find the most up-to-date information you can, so look for the most recent copyright. Remember: it takes about a year for a book to get published, so a current copyright does not guarantee the latest information.

2. *Preface/Foreword.* If this section is written by a noted person in the field, it is a good clue that the book is considered important. The book's contributions might be discussed here along with personal feelings the preface writer may have about the author or subject. Very often, the preface also explains what the book is about, which can give you important clues to its structure and content. The preface may also explain why the book was written, or how it should be used.

Unfortunately, people usually ignore the preface or foreword. "It's just that much more to read," they lament. Make it a habit *always* to read this material. It's an invaluable source of information about the author's background, experience, training, and qualifications. This, in turn, can help you gauge the author's reliability.

3. *Introduction.* Usually written by the author, the introduction describes the book's purpose and content. It also introduces you to the author's writing style. This "sneak preview" can help you become familiar with the author's use of language. This can save you time later on.

4. *Reviewers' comments.* Naturally, the reviewers' comments will be favorable, so focus on what is bring praised and who is doing the praising. What features do the critics single out for accolades? Are these topics that interest you? Then look at the critics' names and their credentials. Are these people well known? Are they affiliated with important universities, scholarly centers, newspapers, or magazines? Are they media figures or accomplished in their own field? What weight do their words carry with you? Reviewers' comments are found on both the opening pages and on the cover.

5. *Table of contents.* This listing provides an invaluable clue to the book's organization. Read the table of contents carefully, paying special attention to the first and last chapters, the introduction and summary. Then spend a few minutes mentally reviewing the method of organization. Skim the opening paragraphs of any chapters that you found confusing, until their method of organization becomes clear. This can prevent you from getting bogged down later on.

By now, you should have a fairly good idea of the book's contents. The whole process should not have taken you more than 10 minutes — perhaps even less with a short book.

End Material

You are almost done with your quick overview—there are just a few sections left. Many books contain end matter as well as prefatory material. Here is some of the most common material you can find at the end of a book. Review it as you would prefatory material.

1. *Appendix.* An appendix usually contains informative materials for the reader that are nonessential to the text. Many types of material can be consigned to appendixes, including illustrations, charts, tables, lengthy lists, and documents.

2. *Glossary.* Some books do not require a list of difficult terms; others do. Consider the book's subject and see if there is a glossary at the back. Is it needed? If it is present, what new information about the book can it give you?

3. *Bibliography.* The style of a bibliography will vary with the type of book. At any rate, it is a listing of sources, many of which will interest the reader.

4. *Index.* An index can save you enormous time when you are looking for some specific bits of information. It may also indicate that the nonfiction book was carefully prepared.

Reading Fiction

The previous method works best with textbooks and nonfiction, the types of books you will read most often for information concerning your occupation or education. Clearly, this method is not as effective with novels, plays, or short stories, works that you read for pleasure. Let's now explore a method to read fiction.

Studies have revealed that most people use speed-reading techniques to deal with the explosion of informational material. They must read this material for their careers or community activities. Fiction, in contrast, is read for pleasure. It offers relaxation from the pressures of nonfiction reading. With fiction, there's nothing to memorize, nothing to take notes on. You just relax and enjoy the escape from the pressures of everyday life.

Since your goal in reading fiction is enjoyment, *don't skim* the text. There is no purpose in knowing what will happen in the book, play, or story before you read it. Skimming might very well spoil the book by giving away the ending! For the same reason, there is no reason to preview most of the text. The only section you might want to read is the *summary* on the book jacket.

Using the Summary

The summary can help you place the main events in order, which will make your reading easier. It can also introduce you to the important characters and when and where the action takes place. Overall, a well-written summary will place information in context without revealing key plot and character twists.

Vary your reading speed depending on the way the material is written. Works by Chaucer, Milton, and Shakespeare, for example, must be read more slowly than contemporary novels with less texture. This is especially true when there are language differences, as in Shakespeare's plays. If you read a number of Shakespeare's plays, you will find that your reading speed picks up, but at first it's apt to be slow going.

But even if you're reading a fictional work written in contemporary English, you're not going to want to rush through it. Aside from giving yourself enough time to appreciate the author's style, you have to allow yourself enough time to digest the book's tone. If the book presents strong feelings, you should be able to enjoy the experience. If you don't have to rush through pleasure reading, sit back and take your time! In the main, then, use speed-reading techniques for materials you must read, so you have more time for materials you want to read.

You Can Read Fiction More Quickly!

What happens if you want to read a novel but you just don't have the time? There *are* some modifications you can make to increase your reading speed, but be aware that you may sacrifice some of the book's quality.

Some authors, both contemporary and time-honored, write long descriptive passages. Usually, these passages describe the setting, mood, or characters. This is especially common in the works of 19th century writers who were paid by the word, such as Charles Dickens. You will also find long descriptive passages in many of the novels by Robert Ludlum, Stephen King, and James Michener. You can speed-read through these passages without sacrificing much of the plot or suspense. The key is to vary your reading rate depending on the content. Follow these steps:

1. Read the topic sentence of the paragraph at your normal reading rate.
2. Skim the paragraphs rich in description. Pick out key nouns and verbs.
3. Focus on important details; skim over minor ones.
4. Savor well-written passages.

Be sure to keep the main events, characters, and settings clearly in mind. As you read, summarize the novel's meaning in your own words. This will help you put all the details in their proper place.

Exercise

Below is a selection from H.G. Wells's *The Time Machine*. Following the steps above, read the selection at your best reading rate, without sacrificing enjoyment. Use a timer to keep track of your reading speed.

The Time Traveler (for so it will be convenient to speak of him) was expounding a recondite matter to us. His gray eyes

shone and twinkled, and his usually pale face was flushed and animated. The fire burned brightly, and the soft radiance of the incandescent lights in the lilies of silver caught the bubbles that flashed and passed in our glasses. Our chairs, being his patents, embraced and caressed us rather than submitted to be sat upon, and there was that luxurious after-dinner atmosphere when thought runs gracefully free of the
10 trammels of precision. And he put it to us in this way—marking the points with a lean forefinger—as we sat and lazily admired his earnestness over this new paradox (as we thought it) and his fecundity.

"You must follow me carefully. I shall have to controvert one or two ideas that are almost universally accepted. The geometry, for instance, they taught you at school is founded on a misconception."

"Is not that rather a large thing to expect us to begin upon?" said Filby, an argumentative person with red hair.

20 "I do no mean to ask you to accept anything without reasonable ground for it. You will soon admit as much as I need from you. You know of course that a mathematical line, a line of thickness *nil,* has no real existence. They taught you that? Neither has a mathematical plane. These things are mere abstraction."

"That is all right," said the Psychologist.

"Nor, having only length, breadth, and thickness, can a cube have a real existence."

"There I object," said Filby. "Of course a solid body may
30 exist. All real things—"

"So most people think. But wait a moment. Can an *instantaneous* cube exist?"

"Don't follow you," said Filby.

"Can a cube that does not last for any time at all, have a real existence?"

Filby became pensive. "Clearly," the Time Traveler

proceeded, "any real body must have extension in *four* directions: it must have Length, Breadth, Thickness, and— Duration. But through a natural infirmity of the flesh, which I
40 will explain to you in a moment, we incline to overlook this fact. There are really four dimensions, three which we call the three planes of Space, and a fourth, Time. There is, however, a tendency to draw an unreal distinction between the former three dimensions and the latter, because it happens that our consciousness moves intermittently in one direction along the latter from the beginning to the end of our lives."

"That," said a very young man, making spasmodic efforts to relight his cigar over the lamp, "that . . . very clear indeed."
50 "Now, it is very remarkable that this is so extensively overlooked," continued the Time Traveler, with a slight accession of cheerfulness. "Really this is what is meant by the Fourth Dimension, though some people who talk about the Fourth Dimension do not know they mean it. It is only another way of looking at Time. *There is no difference between Time and any of the three dimensions of Space except that our consciousness moves along it.* But some foolish people have got hold of the wrong side of that idea. You have all heard what they have to say about this Fourth
60 Dimension?"

"*I* have not," said the Provincial Mayor.

"It is simply this. That Space, as our mathematicians have it, is spoken of as having three dimensions, which one may call Length, Breadth, and Thickness, and is always definable by reference to three planes, each at right angles to the others. But some philosophical people have been asking why *three* dimensions particularly—why not another direction at right angles to the other three?—and have even tried to construct a Four-Dimension geometry. Professor Simon

70 Newcomb was expounding this to the New York
Mathematical Society only a month or so ago. You know
how on a flat surface, which has only two dimensions, we
can represent a figure of a three-dimensional solid, and
similarly they think that by models of three dimensions they
could represent one of four—if they could master the
perspective of the thing. See?"

"I think so," murmured the Provincial Mayor, and knitting
his brows, he lapsed into an introspective state, his lips
moving as one who repeats mystic words. "Yes, I think I see
80 it now," he said after some time, brightening in a quite
transitory manner.

"Well, I do not mind telling you I have been at work upon
this geometry of Four Dimensions for some time. Some of
my results are curious. For instance, here is a portrait of a
man at eight years old, another at fifteen, another at
seventeen, another at twenty-three, and so on. All these are
evidently sections, as it were, Three-Dimensional
representations of his Four-Dimensioned being, which is a
fixed and unalterable thing.

90 "Scientific people," proceeded the Time Traveler, after the
pause required for the proper assimilation of this, "know very
well that Time is only a kind of Space. Here is a popular
scientific diagram, a weather record. This line I trace with my
finger shows the movement of the barometer. Yesterday it
was so high, yesterday night it fell, then this morning it rose
again, and so gently upward to here. Surely the mercury did
not trace this line in any of the dimensions of Space
generally recognized? But certainly it traced such a line, and
that line, therefore, we must conclude was along the Time
100 Dimension."

"But," said the Physician, staring hard at a coal in the fire,
"if Time is really only a fourth dimension of Space, why is it,

and why has it always been, regarded as something different? And why cannot we move in Time as we move about in the other dimensions of Space?"

The Time Traveler smiled. "Are you sure we can move freely in Space? Right and left we can go, backward and forward freely enough, and men always have done so. I admit we move freely in two dimensions. But how about up 110 and down? Gravitation limits us there."

"Not exactly," said the Physician. "There are balloons."

"But before the balloons, save for spasmodic jumping and the inequalities of the surface, humanity had no freedom of vertical movement."

"Still they could move a little up and down," said the Physician.

"Easier, far easier down than up."

"And you cannot move at all in Time, you cannot get away from the present moment."

120 "My dear sir, that is just where you are wrong. That is just where the whole world has gone wrong. We are always getting away from the present movement. Our mental existences, which are immaterial and have no dimensions, are passing along the Time Dimension with a uniform velocity from the cradle to the grave. Just as we should travel *down* if we began our existence fifty miles above the earth's surface."

Reading rate: _____

LESSON FIVE: READING LETTERS WITH EASE

Buried in résumés and letters? Can't get through your business communications? If you get only a handful of letters a day, you will most likely read them all completely. But if you are like most overworked businesspeople, you get too many letters every day to read them all. Below are some possible letters that you might receive. How many more can you add to the list?

- letters soliciting donations
- letters of introduction
- sales orders
- job application letters
- credit letters
- thank-you letters
- business promotion letters
- letters asking for information
- adjustment letters
- letters of complaint

Here's a surefire method for tripling your reading speed with business letters.

---

8 Steps to Speed-Reading Your Correspondence

1. First, practice what you preach! Don't send a business letter unless you absolutely have to! Of course, there are many times when you will have to communicate by mail, but try to limit your business correspondence to necessary letters. This will save time for you, your support staff, and your business contacts. Use E-mail more often, to save time.

2. Now to the mail. First, skim all the return addresses on the *envelopes* to find out who sent the letters.

3. Don't assume that you have to read all the letters. If the letter is of no interest, discard it unopened. Many busy executives dispose of vast quantities of junk mail without opening any of it!

4. Skim the letterheads of the mail you open. Quickly ascertain the relative importance of each letter.

5. Then sort the letters into three piles — most important, important, and least important — according to the information on the letterheads.

6. *Most important letters:* Read these all the way through; they deserve your full attention. Use your fastest reading speed.

7. *Important letters:* Read the *second and last paragraphs* only. The first paragraph is less important because it contains the complimentary opening. The second paragraph is important because it contains the "meat" of the letter. The final paragraph is important because the facts should be reiterated and there should be a call for action. Skim the entire letter if these two sections are unclear.

8. *Least important letters:* Read the *last paragraphs* to find out what action you are required to take. Skim the second paragraph if the final paragraph is unclear.

Exercise

Read this business letter and answer the questions that follow.

ARDA Sheetmetal Fabricators
855 Third Avenue
Brooklyn, NY 10094

June 15, 1994

Ms. Carol Stephenson, Director
Spring Valley Public Library
Bluepoint Lane
Spring Valley, NY 13345

Dear Ms. Stephenson:

Thank you for your letter of June 10, 1994. I have checked personally into the matter you raised. In addition, I passed your letter on to the drafting department, and to library liaison, Mia Callebro.

According to your letter, at the last field meeting, the library and architect agreed to reconfigure the heating system to reduce the overall HVAC cost. Our representative could not be present at that meeting, so we did not know about the changes until we received your letter. We cannot implement the reconfigured heating ducts until we receive an official change order. Please send us a change order to approve the reconfiguration you requested. We have enclosed a prepaid overnight mailer to expedite this matter. Or you may fax us the change order at 918-555-3477.

Thank you for your time and attention to this matter. We are sorry for any inconvenience and misunderstanding.

Sincerely,

Joe Perez, President
ARDA Sheetmetal Fabricators

cc: Mia Callebro.

Questions

1. Why is Mr. Perez writing this letter? _____

   _____

2. What action is called for on Ms. Stephenson's part? _____

   _____

3. Which paragraph is the most important? Why? _____

   _____

4. Did you have to read this entire letter? Why or why not?

_____

_____

Answers

1. He wants a change order to confirm changes in the library's new heating system.
2. She must send the change order, via the mailer or fax.
3. The second paragraph is the most important; it contains the key information.
4. You did not have to read the entire letter to understand what it said, because the key information was in the second paragraph.

Exercise

Read the following business letter and answer the questions.

NEW LOOK
CONSUMER AFFAIRS
PO BOX 101
YOUNG AMERICA, MN 89112

Ms. Aysha Johnson
83 Longacre Drive
Greenlawn, NJ 07064

Dear Ms. Johnson:

We are sorry to hear about the problems you had with our "Twice as Nice" hair coloring. You explained that the coloring agent was difficult to apply and, as a result, caused damage to your towels and rugs. Thank you for taking the time to write to us about your concerns.

For us to assist you further, please send us the product, the damaged items, and receipts or estimates of replacement costs. For your convenience, we are enclosing a prepaid label. Please attach it to the package.

We will do our best to resolve this situation promptly. Thank you for giving us the opportunity to help you in this matter. Customer satisfaction is our number one concern.

Sincerely,

Aleece Washington
Consumer Affairs

Enclosure
99087565-4

Questions

1. Why is Ms. Washington writing this letter? _____

   _____

2. What does Ms. Washington want Ms. Johnson to do? __

   _____

3. Which paragraph is the most important? Why? _____

   _____

Answers

1. She is writing in response to Ms. Johnson's complaints about the company's hair coloring.

2. Ms. Washington wants Ms. Johnson to send the rest of the hair coloring, any damaged items, and receipts or estimates of replacement costs.

3. The second paragraph is the most important; it contains the key information.

LESSON SIX: READING SPECIAL-INTEREST MATERIAL

In addition to reading for your job and for pleasure, you may have occasion to read special-interest materials. These materials could be magazines, books, pamphlets, or operating manuals. They might concern hobbies like computers, home repair, auto restoration, fishing, stamp and coin collecting, knitting, sewing, collecting antiques, sailing, flying, cooking, or gardening. Reading this kind of material is similar to, yet different from, other kinds of reading you do.

Like work-related reading, special-interest reading requires you to extract information. But unlike reading for your career, special-interest reading is usually done at your own pace to meet personal goals. And like pleasure reading, it is done for enjoyment. But unlike reading a novel, short story, or play, reading for a hobby requires you to come away with very specialized knowledge and information. You can't skim description here, for even minor details might prove very important later on.

Here are some suggestions for speeding up special-interest reading:

1. Skim the text to preview the contents. Find sections that will give you the most information for your time. Look for:
   - summaries
   - graphs
   - illustrations
   - author bios
   - table of contents
   - diagrams
   - photographs
   - charts

2. Read the material at your fastest reading rate. Speed up when you come across information you do *not* need. Slow down when you come across information you *do* need.
3. Mark important points in the margin of the text. Use a pencil and code your marks. For example, use a line or star to show a key point, and a question mark to indicate a confusing passage.
4. Return to the text and analyze any passages you have marked. Since you may be coming to much of the material with ample prior knowledge, you may not have many places marked to reread.

This method is especially useful for learning new computer programs when you have to wade through complicated software documentation. But it also works well with any hobby reading, such as the two selections below.

Exercise

The following selection is on stamp collecting, one of the most popular hobbies around the world. Read the selection and use the method described above. Don't forget to time yourself so you can record your reading rate.

United States Postal Service

Souvenir cards have been issued by the U.S. Postal Service and its predecessor, the U.S. Post Office Department, since 1960. They are generally issued for international philatelic exhibitions outside the United States or for special domestic occasions.

The forerunner of the U.S. souvenir card was the 1938 issue by the U.S. Post Office Department in conjunction with the philatelic truck that toured the United States from 1939 to

10 1941. It was a blue-and-white 3-by-4 1/2-inch card showing the White House. Over 750,000 copies were printed and distributed nationwide. The last copies were printed on ungummed stock, after the gummed issues began to appear affixed in unwanted places apparently by the original purchasers, throughout the country.

Current records and information provide more figures regarding the quantity of those souvenir cards issued. Officially, 187,000 gummed cards and 579,500 ungummed cards were issued. These figures are probably more

20 accurate in accounting for actual numbers in circulation.

All cards after this earliest pictorial one measure six by eight inches. The cards issued for foreign exhibitions are generally distributed free to patrons at these exhibitions. Until 1976, the mint price for a card in the United States was $1, then the price increased to $1.25. As of 1980, the price was about $2 for a mint card. Canceled cards were also offered, starting in 1976, franked with U.S. postage and canceled with the special U.S. Postal Service show cancellation for the event being noted. Canceled cards are

30 generally priced at the cost of mint cards, plus the cost of stamps used in franking. Mail orders are subject to a $5 minimum, and a 50¢ handling charge per order. Orders should be mailed to

Philatelic Sales Branch
U.S. Postal Service
Washington, DC 20265

Although there are no specific time limits imposed on souvenir card orders, most cards are removed from sale within approximately one year from the date of issue. Some

40 may remain on sale longer, and others may be withdrawn sooner, especially if stock becomes depleted. U.S. Postal Service policy on future issues may be subject to change.

Reading rate: _____

Exercise

Here's a passage on a more esoteric hobby — flying. Use the method you just learned as you read this selection. Be sure to time yourself so you can record your reading rate. Compare the rate at which you read this passage with the rate at which you read the previous one. See if your rate improved through practice.

Principles of Flight

There are certain laws of nature or physics that apply to any object that is lifted from the earth and moved through the air. To analyze and predict airplane performance under various operating conditions, it is important that pilots gain as much knowledge as possible concerning the laws and principles that apply to flight.

The principles of flight discussed in this chapter are intended primarily for beginning pilots, and are not intended
10 as detailed and complete explanations of the complexities of aerodynamics. However, this information should encourage interested individuals to further their study.

Forces Acting on the Airplane in Flight

When it is in flight, there are certain favorable forces and other unfavorable forces acting on the airplane. It is the primary task of the pilot to control these forces so as to direct the airplane's speed and flight path in a safe and efficient manner. To do this, the pilot must understand these forces and their effects.

20 Among the aerodynamic forces acting on an airplane during flight, four are considered to be basic because they act upon it during all maneuvers. These basics are *lift,* the upward-acting force; *weight* (or gravity), the downward-acting force; *thrust,* the forward-acting force; and *drag,* the rearward-acting, or retarding, force.

While in a steady-state flight, the altitude, direction, and
speed of the airplane will remain constant until one or more
of the basic forces changes in magnitude. In unaccelerated
flight (steady flight), the opposing forces are in equilibrium.
30 Life and thrust are considered as positive forces (+), while
weight and drag are considered as negative forces (–); the
sum of the opposing forces is zero. In other words, lift equals
weight and thrust equals drag.

When pressure is applied to airplane controls, one or
more of the basic forces changes in magnitude and
becomes greater than the opposing force, causing the
airplane to accelerate or move in the direction of the applied
force. For example, if power is applied (increasing thrust)
and altitude is maintained, the airplane will accelerate. As
40 speed increases, drag increases, until a point is reached
where drag again equals thrust, and the airplane will
continue in steady flight at a higher speed. As another
example, if power is applied while in level flight, the climb
forward is established and the force of lift will increase during
the time back elevator pressure is applied; after a steady-
state climb is established, the force of lift will be
approximately equal to the force of weight. The airplane
does not climb because lift is greater than in level flight, but
because thrust is greater than drag, and because a
50 component of thrust is developed that acts upward,
perpendicular to the flight path.

Airplane designers make an effort to increase the
performance of the airplane by increasing the efficiency of
the desirable forces of lift and thrust while reducing, as much
as possible, the undesirable forces of weight and drag.
Nonetheless, compromise must be made to satisfy the
function and desired performance of the airplane.

Reading rate: _____

LESSON SEVEN: STUDYING MORE EFFECTIVELY

Studying is different from other kinds of reading because you usually have to remember the information for only a short time. Naturally, you want to retain the overall outlines of your reading, but you most often need to recall for only a finite time — until a test is over, for example. And studying involves additional steps, including

- recalling
- learning
- memorizing.

As a basic rule, read as fast as you can to locate important material. Then learn the material. Your time should be divided as follows:

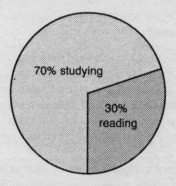

Here are the steps to follow when studying:

1. Begin by skimming the material you have to study. Allocate about 15–20 minutes for this — no more! The purpose of studying is to learn the material, not the text layout, so skim only what you need to know to get the orientation of the material. If you are reading a textbook, pay special attention to the following features:

- chapter heads
- graphics
- summaries
- table of contents
- glossary
- abstracts

2. Read the text at your most comfortable rate. Look for information that most directly relates to the subject of the upcoming text.
3. If you own the text, mark important places with a pencil. Be sure to isolate those that will require additional study.

Below are several passages for you to use to learn how to use super reading to study effectively. Read each passage, using the three guidelines described above. Then take the tests that follow to see how much material you retained.

Exercise 1

Heart to Heart

The amount of blood pumped by the heart is staggering. When you are at complete rest, your heart pumps enough blood to fill four automobile gasoline tanks each hour. During rest, the heart beats about 70 times per minute. During each beat, each side pumps nearly 70 ml of blood. The amount of blood pumped during each minute is, then, almost 5 liters, or over 5 quarts, per minute.

The amount of blood pumped by each side of the heart
10 during each minute is called the "cardiac output." During activity, the cardiac output changes. When you exercise, your cardiac output can rise to as much as 25 liters per minute. When a trained athlete exercises, his or her output may be as high as 40 liters per minute.

The cardiac output is controlled in part by nerves in the autonomic nervous system. Impulses carried by sympathetic nerves in the heart tend to increase cardiac output by

increasing both the rate of the heartbeat and the strength of
each beat. Impulses carried by the parasympathetic nerves
20 to the heart tend to decrease cardiac output by slowing the
rate of heartbeat.

Questions

1. What is the resting heartbeat? _____

   _____

2. How much blood does each side of the heart pump dur-

   ing each beat? _____

3. How much blood does the heart pump per minute? _____

   _____

4. What is the "cardiac output"? _____

   _____

5. Is the cardiac output constant? _____

6. What controls the cardiac output? _____

   _____

Answers

1. It is about 70 times per minute.
2. It pumps nearly 70 ml of blood.
3. It pumps almost 5 liters, or over 5 quarts, per minute.
4. It is the amount of blood pumped by each side of the
   heart per minute.
5. No, it is not.
6. The cardiac output is controlled in part by nerves in the
   autonomic nervous system.

Exercise 2

Immigration Requirements

Persons arriving from a foreign country (including Canada) must report for immigration inspection immediately upon arrival in the United States.

With few exceptions, all persons who are not U.S. citizens or permanent resident aliens are required to present a visa upon entering the United States. Visas can be obtained only at a U.S. consulate or embassy abroad. Canadian citizens are exempt from visa requirements in most cases.

10   U.S. and Canadian citizens are advised to carry proof of citizenship, which may be a passport, birth certificate, naturalization papers, or other documents that support the claimed citizenship. A driver's license is not proof of citizenship. Most aliens are required to present a valid, unexpired passport. If you are in doubt as to what documents are required for entry, call the nearest U.S. consulate or embassy, or U.S. Immigration and Naturalization Service (INS) office.

Most aliens must execute and present Form I-94,
20   Arrival/Departure Record. INS has revised Form I-94, effective March 1, 1986, and prior editions may not be used. Form I-94 must be completed by all persons except U.S. citizens, returning resident aliens, aliens with immigrant visas, and Canadians visiting or in transit. Mexican nationals in possession of Immigration Form I-86 or Form I-586 are exempted from Form I-94 reporting requirements when their destination is California, Arizona, New Mexico, or Texas, and the stay will not exceed 72 hours. This exemption does not apply when travel will be beyond 25 miles from the
30   international border between Mexico and the United States. Travel to Nevada by Mexican nationals is exempted for periods of less than 30 days. Mexican nationals proceeding

to destinations more than 25 miles from the border of the states named above will have to obtain Visitors Permit I-444 when arriving in the United States. Mexican nationals presenting official or diplomatic passports and entering the United States for purposes other than permanent assignment are exempted from Form I-94 reporting requirements.

Questions

1. When do people arriving from a foreign place have to report to Immigration? _____

2. What proof do people who are not U.S. citizens or permanent resident aliens have to present at Immigration?

   _____

   _____

3. Name three different documents that prove citizenship.

   _____

   _____

4. Is a driver's license alone proof of citizenship? _____

5. What agencies can you contact if you do not know what documents to present for entry? _____

   _____

6. When are Mexican nationals exempted from Form I-94 reporting requirements? _____

   _____

Answers

1. They must report immediately upon arrival in the United States.
2. They must present a visa.
3. Proof includes passports, birth certificates, or naturalization papers.
4. No, it is not.
5. If you are in doubt as to what documents are required for entry, call the nearest U.S. consulate, embassy, or U.S. Immigration and Naturalization Service office.
6. They are exempt when their destination is limited to California, Arizona, New Mexico, or Texas, and the stay will not exceed 72 hours.

LESSON EIGHT: READING OFF COMPUTER SCREENS

With the 21st century technology explosion, the chances are great that more and more of your reading will be off computers, not from printed sources. Increasingly, employees in all fields are writing and editing memos, letters, reports, and other documents on-line, or reviewing on-screen texts that others have generated. Further, you will very likely use computerized information retrieval services to access data. In some instances, you will be able to print out a hard copy of something that appears on your computer screen or receive a copy through fax. There are other instances, however, when time and economic constraints will make a hard copy impossible. It might take too long to generate a copy, for example, or printers might not interface properly. With on-line information retrieval services, it is especially likely that you will be charged extra for generating a hard copy. In these cases, you will have to read off the computer screen directly—and fast! If you are being charged for access time, you will want to read the material as quickly and as accurately as possible. While you can adapt the speed-reading skills you learned for technical materials to reading from a computer screen, there are some special methods for increasing your reading speed when working on-line. Let's look at them now.

Tricks of the Trade

Here are some ways that video display terminal (VDT) professionals maximize their reading speed and comprehension.

- **Contrast.** People who use VDTs a great deal of the time realize that high screen contrast can make reading from computers much easier. Users are divided, however, over the advantages of black-and-white versus color monitors. As recently as five years ago, contrast was decidedly better on black-and-white monitors, because they provided the sharpest visuals. Orange-on-black type is especially easy on the eyes. Recent innovations with color monitors have evened the score, though. Since many of the newest software programs will not run on black-and-white monitors, if you have state-of-the-art equipment, you will most likely be working on a color monitor. But if you have an older black-and-white screen, you will not be at a disadvantage.

  In either case, adjust the contrast and brightness until you achieve the greatest possible screen clarity. This is not a one-time setting! As the light varies in your office throughout the day, you should adjust the contrast to compensate.
- **Lighting.** The lighting in your workstation can greatly affect how fast and well you read off the screen. A glare on the screen, for instance, can make reading much harder. A common misconception is that natural light is best for computer work. This is not always so! As a matter

of fact, natural light can be uneven and create a lot of glare on the screen. Try not to have your terminal against a window, and use shades or blinds to make the outside lighting as comfortable as possible. By all means have a light over the screen, but use a low-wattage bulb to reduce glare. Experiment with various combinations of natural and artificial light to achieve the illumination that makes on-screen reading easiest.

- **Eyestrain.** While any reading can create eyestrain, reading off a computer screen can be especially tiring. In addition to eye fatigue, you may experience cramped shoulders, a stiff neck, sore arms, and other physical strain. In large part, this is because you are working in one position. When you are reading from hard copy, in contrast, it is much easier to vary your position. As a result, it is especially important for maximizing speed and comprehension that you look up from the screen every 15 minutes or so. Take a few seconds to look at the horizon and focus on objects in the room. Don't skip these breaks! They will help you keep up your reading speed by reducing strain.

On-Line Speed-Reading

New technology calls for new reading tools. Here are four on-line speed-reading methods that professionals find especially useful.

1. **Use the line spacer.** It's obviously cumbersome to use you hand to guide your reading on screen. Your arm will cramp within moments. Instead, use the line spacer. Press on the "down" arrow with your right hand as you read. Like the hand motions you learned earlier, this forces your eye to move as quickly as it can through the text, taking in larger "bytes" of type! Practice this technique until your hand–eye coordination is smooth.

2. **Use the "page down" key.** You know that the best way to read faster is to read more words at a time. This is even easier to do on a computer. As you pick up speed, switch from the line spacer to the "page down" key. You will find this key on the right-hand side of most keyboards. Using this key forces your eyes to skim entire pages of type in one swoop.

3. **Single-spaced text.** Very often, you have a choice of single-, double-, or even triple-spaced text. If you have a choice, opt for single-spaced text, because it packs the most information for the punch. This makes it easier — and faster — to read on-screen.

4. **Type face.** Finally, read and edit in the simplest possible type face if you have a choice. Most word-processing programs can create beautiful fonts. While attractive, these are very distracting and will greatly slow your reading and understanding. You can always convert the text to another font before printing.

7

Common Reading Problems and How to Solve Them

You would expect that average readers would move their eyes smoothly across the page, or follow one of the simple eye patterns that help them increase their reading speed and comprehension. This is not the case! The average reader wastes a tremendous amount of time looking up, across, and below the text. This wasted eye motion costs valuable reading time. The distractions affect comprehension, too. In this chapter, you will learn about the most common reading problems and ways to solve them.

People slow their reading time through three common wasted eye motions:

- *Regressions:* moving their eyes back over text they have already read
- *Progressions:* looking forward to text before they are ready to read it
- *Distractions:* looking away from the text

LESSON ONE: BEATING VISUAL REGRESSIONS

When you're reading a text at super speed, you may miss key words and phrases. In these cases, it's tempting to look back over the text to clarify meaning.

It's not a bad idea to look back occasionally to confirm meaning. The key word here is *occasionally*. Looking back once in a while, especially when you're reading a difficult passage, is not necessarily bad. It can become a problem, however, when it happens too often.

Remember that you don't have to understand every single word to grasp the author's meaning. As you learned earlier, the meaning of a text is often contained in its entirety. You might have to read the entire passage before you understand the author's point. This is very common in fiction, for example, as authors frequently withhold information to create suspense and tension. But you also learned that by reading key nouns and verbs, you can often easily grasp the essence of a passage.

Follow these steps to help overcome problems with visual regressions:

1. With a pencil, mark passages that you found confusing.
2. Don't go back over the passage — keep reading! You will often find that the meaning will become clear.
3. When you finish the entire text, go back over the passages you marked, if you require further clarification.

Exercise

Following the three-step format outlined above, read the following passage. Be sure to keep track of your reading rate with a timer.

A rumor of some unaccountable phenomenon had preceded Mr. Hooper into the meetinghouse, and set all the congregation astir. Few could refrain from twisting their heads toward the door; many stood upright, and turned directly about; several little boys clambered upon the seats, and came down again with a terrible racket. There was a general bustle, a rustling of the women's gowns and shuffling of the men's feet, greatly at variance with that hushed repose that should attend the entrance of a minister.

10 But Mr. Hooper did not notice the perturbation of his people. He entered with an almost noiseless step, bent his head mildly at the pews on either side, and bowed as he passed his oldest parishioner, a white-haired great-grandsire, who occupied an armchair in the center of the aisle. It was strange to observe how slowly this venerable man became conscious of something singular in the appearance of his pastor. He seemed not fully to partake of the prevailing wonder, until Mr. Hooper ascended the stairs and showed himself in the pulpit, face to face with his congregation

20 except for the black veil. That mysterious emblem was never once withdrawn. It shook with his measured breath as he gave out the psalm; it threw its obscurity between him and the holy page as he read the Scriptures; and while he prayed, the veil lay heavily on his uplifted countenance. Did he seek to hide it from the dread Being whom he was addressing? . . .

The next day, the whole village of Milford talked of little else than Parson Hooper's black veil. That, and the mystery that it concealed, supplied a topic for discussion between

30 acquaintances meeting in the street. It was the first item of news that the tavern keeper told his guests. The children babbled of it on their way to school. One imitative little imp covered his face with an old black handkerchief, thereby so affrighting his playmates that the panic seized himself, and he well-nigh lost his wits by his own waggery.

Reading rate: _____

LESSON TWO: CONQUERING VISUAL PROGRESSIONS

Not only do readers look back over text they have already read, they also look ahead to glance at words, pictures, and photographs in the text. This is not the same as previewing a text!

You know that it is a very good idea to leaf through a book to get an idea of its contents. This preview technique can save you valuable reading time. But looking ahead while you are reading can also cost you time. Visual progressions cut back on reading speed without adding anything to comprehension. How can you cut back on visual progressions? Follow these steps:

1. Thoroughly preview the text. Look at all the illustrations, photographs, maps, graphs, charts, and so on.
2. When you are familiar with the book's visual features, you will be less likely to want to skip ahead.

Exercise

Following the steps described above, read the following passage. Be sure to keep track of your reading rate with a timer. Beware of the illustration! Be sure to preview the text so you are not distracted by the drawing.

Workstation Compatibility and Design

In the office environment, the workstation consists primarily of a work surface of some sort, a chair, a VDT, and other related items (see Figure 1).

The employee must have adequate space to perform each of the tasks required by the job. Individual body size must be considered, and will influence the design of the chair, the height of the work surface, and access to various elements of the workstation, including the display screen.

10   A height-adjustable work surface is an advantage. In
general, a good VDT work surface will provide as many
adjustable features as possible. Also, adequate leg room
should be provided for the employee to stretch out and
relieve some of the static load that results from sitting with
the legs in a fixed position for a long time.

Chair

The chair can be a crucial factor in preventing adverse
health effects as well as improving employee performance in
office work. Since the majority of office workers spend most
20 of their time sitting, proper back and shoulder support help
reduce fatigue. If the chair does not fit the worker properly,
there can be serious physical effects, as well as effects on
performance. As a result, the appropriate types of ergonomic
chairs should be made available to accommodate various
worker needs.

Chair Height

When an employee must spend from six to eight hours
seated, the heights of the chair and the work surface are
crucial. The human body dimension that provides a starting
30 point for determining correct chair height is the "popliteal"
height. This is the height from the floor to the point at the
crease behind the knee. The chair height is correct when the
entire sole of the foot can rest on the floor or footrest and
back of the knee is slightly higher than the seat of the chair.
This allows the blood to circulate freely in the legs and feet.

Seatpan Design

Size and shape are two factors to consider in the design
of the seatpan of the chair. The seatpan can be slightly
concave with a rounded or "waterfall" edge. This will help
40 distribute the weight and may prevent sliding forward in the

chair. The angle of the seatpan should also be considered. Some options include a seatpan that slopes slightly down at the back or one that has a forward tilt that produces less stress on the lower back.

Backrest

A proper backrest should support the entire back, including the lower region. The seat and backrest of the chair should support a comfortable posture that permits frequent variations in the sitting position. The backrest angle
50 and chair height should be easily adjustable. A footrest may be necessary for shorter individuals.

Reading rate: _____

LESSON THREE: OVERCOMING
VISUAL DISTRACTIONS

It is not hard to be distracted from reading, especially when the text is not particularly interesting! But it is becoming increasingly acknowledged by professionals as well as the general public that concentrating can help people accomplish difficult tasks much more easily. Through biofeedback techniques, people can learn to lower their blood pressure, relieve stress, and relax. Many meditation techniques accomplish the same results.

One of the best ways to stay focused on the text is to use the hand motions you learned at the beginning of the book. The motion of your hands over the text can help you avoid visual distractions. Below is a focusing exercise that super readers use to help them avoid visual distractions.

1. Sit in a comfortable chair in a quiet room.
2. Close your eyes and think of any single-digit number.
3. When your mind begins to wander, think of another single-digit number.
4. Continue this for 15 minutes.

8

Self Tests

Now it's time to put it all together! Apply what you know to the following selections. Try to read as quickly and accurately as you can, using the techniques you learned in this book. Then answer the questions that follow each passage to test your comprehension.

Passage 1:
Days of Wine and Roses

Wine is an alcoholic beverage made from the juice of fresh, ripe grapes. There are five main classes of wine, and each is made differently. Wine producers classify the wines according to when they are served and for what purpose. For example, there are aperitif wines, red table wines, rosé (pink) table wines, white table wines, and sparkling dessert wines.

The winemaking process begins at the harvest, during the late summer or early fall. During the harvest, the grapes
10 are picked and sent to the winery. At the winery, the grapes are mechanically crushed and the juice pumped into large

tanks called "vats." While the grape juice is in the vat, it undergoes a process called "fermentation."

During fermentation, the sugar in the grape juice is converted by yeast into carbon dioxide and alcohol. During this time, the color of the wine is determined. To make red wine, the skins of the grapes are added to the juice while it ferments. The pigment in the skins gives the wine its deep, rich color. To make a light pink rosé wine, the skins are
20 added to the vats for a short time. White wine is created by eliminating all skins from the vat during fermentation.

To produce a dry wine, fermentation must be completed. Sweet or aperitif wines undergo a shorter fermentation. A second fermentation period is used to create sparkling wines. After fermentation, wines are aged in storage casks to develop flavor. The aging period can be months or even years. The amount of time depends on the type of wine being made and the quality of the grape. The wine is switched from cask to cask to get rid of any solid debris that
30 may have collected at the bottom of the cask.

After the wine is properly aged, it is filtered and placed in glass bottles. The bottles are stored in dark, cool places. Corked wine bottles are stored on their sides so that the bottles remain airtight and the cork stays moist.

Salut!

Reading rate: _____

Questions

1. How many classes of wine are produced today? _____

2. How are wines classified? _____

_____

3. Name two different kinds of wine: _____

_____

4. When does the winemaking process begin? _____

_____

5. What happens to the grapes during fermentation? ____

_____

6. What determines the color of the wine? _____

_____

7. How is red wine made? _____

_____

8. What produces a dry wine? _____

_____

9. How are sparkling wines created? _____

_____

10. What happens to the wine after fermentation is completed?

_____

_____

11. Why is wine switched from cask to cask? _____

_____

_____

12. What happens to the wine after it is aged? _____

_____

_____

Answers

1. There are six.
2. They are classified according to when they are served and for what purpose.
3. Possible answers: aperitif wines, red table wines, rosé (pink) table wines, white table wines, and sparkling dessert wines
4. It begins at harvest.
5. The sugar in the grape juice is converted by yeast into carbon dioxide and alcohol.
6. The presence or absence of grape skins during fermentation.
7. The skins of the grapes are added to the juice while it ferments.
8. It is produced by complete fermentation.
9. A second fermentation period is used to create sparkling wines.
10. It is aged in storage casks to develop flavor.
11. It is switched from cask to cask to get rid of any solid debris that may have collected at the bottom of the cask.
12. It is filtered and placed in glass bottles.

Passage 2:
Electronic Publishing

Document Quality

Currently, work is being conducted to produce a standard page description language, SPDL. This language will be device-independent and enable a document represented in SPDL to be output to any display or printing device. It will be capable of representing all types of information, intermixed in any way, as well as black-and-white, multilevel monochrome, or full-color documents. Moreover, the SPDL

10 will neutralize any output device differences that may affect the quality of the document.

Electronic publishing systems have provided users with the technology to design and produce high-quality, aesthetically pleasing documents. However, having the technology does not guarantee quality results. Producing quality results requires knowledge and skills in such areas as page design, graphic arts, and typography. This is not to say that the user is incapable of producing good-looking documents. Rather, the potential for producing low-quality,
20 aesthetically unsatisfactory documents exists. Moreover, since everyone has his or her own idea of what looks good, the same type of document may have several different looks, each reflecting the artistic taste of the producer. This inconsistency among documents prevents readers from differentiating documents by their format. The two documents on the next two pages illustrate our point.

One method to ensure document quality is to establish a publication style and require everyone to use it. Publication styles, often called templates or style sheets, are created for
30 a class of documents (e.g., memoranda, technical manuals, executive summaries, product catalogs). The basic premise of a publication style is the separation of the document content from its layout and format. The author or artist creates the content, and a document designer controls the design. Tags, markup, or styles represent the various elements of the document (e.g., paragraphs, headings, subheadings, bulleted items). Associated with each tag are formatting specifications such as:

- font and font size
40 - margins
- alignment
- indentation
- vertical spacing

February 29, 1993

<u>MEMORANDUM</u>

TO: All staff Members
FM: Personnel

RE: Work Schedules

    All staff will report to work on Monday
according to schedule A.

- tabs
- columns
- rules
- boxes
- pagination parameters
- graphic placement preferences.
50   The use of publication styles should be considered for
documents that
- are structured
- reuse the same design
- separate the design and editorial responsibilities
- require a consistent look.

    The international and proposed federal standard,
Standard Generalized Markup Language (SGML), is another
method to ensure document quality. Although SGML is not a
publication style, it can provide the same effect. SGML is

February 29, 1993

To: All staff Members
From: Personnel
Subject: Work Schedules

All staff will report to work on *Monday* according
to <u>Schedule A</u>

---

60 more comprehensive than a publication style. It provides a
syntax for describing the content and structural elements of
a document through markup and the document type
definition (i.e., a definition of all document elements and their
relationships). Formatting specifications are associated with
the markup when the document is processed by a publishing
system or formatter.

Document Management

The publishing process is often divided among several
people and across several departments. This distributed
70 approach can make managing the production process
difficult. Successful document management starts with a
management plan. Taking into account all phases of the
document development cycle, the plan should at least
 • define the work flow and job responsibilities

- establish file names and organization conventions so that information can be known and shared among contributors
- specify revision methods and control
- specify the job tracking information that is desired and the method by which tracking will be accomplished

80 Document management tools can aid in managing the process by

- tracking the information work flow
- tracking the status of the project
- providing revision control and audit trail of all changes and annotations
- provide file management capabilities, including retrieval of documents by key words, dates, and other criteria, preview images at low resolution (to conform identity), and file security and access control

90 These tools may be part of the publishing software or a separate software utility. Most minicomputer-based publishing systems (such as Context, Interleaf, HyperScribe) have built-in document management tools. However, until recently, dedicated document management tools were unavailable for desktop systems. Typically, the document manager and contributors would track the management documents either manually, using job tickets, status reports, and the like, or electronically, using database or spreadsheet software. Today, document management tools are included 100 in desktop systems (such as IMSI PagePerfect) and are available from third-party vendors (ODMS/Matrix and New Riders Publisher's Desktop Manager).

The use of document management tools should be considered for publishing applications that

- involve multiple people and/or multiple organizations
- consist of several document pieces
- undergo extensive review and revision cycles.

Reading rate: _____

Questions

1. What is SPDL? _____

2. What are some advantages of SPDL? _____

_____

_____

3. What is needed to produce high-quality results? _____

_____

_____

4. Describe one way to ensure document quality. _____

_____

_____

5. What is the basic premise of a publication style? _____

_____

_____

6. List six formatting specifications:

_____   _____

_____   _____

_____   _____

7. Under what circumstances should you use publication
   styles? _____

_____

_____

_____

_____

8. What is SGML? How is it used? _____

_____

_____

9. How do you begin successful document management?

_____

_____

10. List two ways that document management tools can aid
    the managing process. _____

_____

_____

11. Do most microcomputer-based publishing systems have
    built-in management tools? _____

12. Do most desktop publishing systems have built-in man-
    agement tools? _____

13. List two conditions for using document management
    tools. _____

_____

_____

14. Explain one thing you learned about document quality
    from this article. _____

_____

_____

Answers

1. It is a standard page description language.
2. It operates independently of the computer, and it can be output, displayed, or printed on any device. It will be capable of representing all types of information, as well as black-and-white, monochrome, or color documents. Moreover, the SPDL will neutralize any output device differences that may affect the quality of the document.
3. You need knowledge and skills in such areas as page design, graphic arts, and typography.
4. Establish a publication style and require everyone to use it.
5. It separates the document content from its layout and format.
6. Possible responses include font and font size, margins, alignment, indentation, vertical spacing, tabs, columns, rules, boxes, pagination parameters, and graphic placement preferences.
7. When the documents are structured, reuse the same design, separate the design and editorial responsibilities, and require a consistent look.
8. Standard Generalized Markup Language, SGML, is another method to ensure document quality. It provides a syntax for describing the content and structural elements of a document.
9. Successful document management starts with a management plan.
10. Possible answers include track information work flow, track project status, provide revision control and audit trail, provide file management capabilities.
11. Yes.
12. Yes.
13. Use them for publishing applications that involve multiple people and/or multiple organizations, consist of sev-

eral document pieces, and undergo extensive review and revision cycles.

14. Answers will vary.

Passage 3:
Centers for Commercial Development

The establishment by NASA of 16 centers for commercial development of space (CCDS) is among the most important steps taken to date to encourage greater involvement by the U.S. private sector in space.

Large and Small Businesses Unite

A number of Fortune 500 industrial firms and scores of small businesses have become affiliated with these innovative research and development centers, which
10 combine the support of government with the talent of American universities and the commercial interests and investments of U.S. industry.

Through one of these centers, the Center for Macromolecular Crystallography at the University of Alabama–Birmingham, a group of pharmaceutical companies is investigating the potential of space-grown protein crystals to support new drug research. The industrial participants in protein crystal growth have been able to fly samples of interest to them on several space shuttle flights.
20 The corporate participants at other CCDS centers are also expected to gain access to spaceflight opportunities through a new agreement mechanism known as the pre-joint endeavor agreement.

Ongoing Research

The centers have continued their research in these areas. They have been working on advanced materials, space remote sensing, space processing, automation and robotics, space propulsion, bioscience, and space power.

BREAKTHROUGH IN SUPERCONDUCTIVITY

30   In late 1986, researchers associated with two of NASA's CCDS centers announced a breakthrough in superconductivity. In conjunction with research on the use of the vacuum of space for producing semiconductor materials, Dr. Paul Chu, of the University of Houston CCDS, and Dr. Mau Wu, of the University of Alabama–Huntsville CCDS, successfully raised the temperature at which material becomes superconductive. Another advance was reported by Dr. Chu in early 1988.

Funding from Various Sources

40   NASA provides annual funding of up to about $1 million for each CCDS, which receives additional financial and in-kind contributions from industrial affiliates that, on the average, exceed the NASA funding. NASA support for the centers is expected to continue until they can become fully established and self-sufficient.

CCDS Centers

    Centers focusing on materials research and processing include the Center for Advanced Materials, Battelle Columbus Laboratories, Columbus, Ohio; the Consortium for
50 Materials Development in Space, University of Alabama–Huntsville; the Center for Macromolecular Crystallography, University of Alabama–Birmingham; Center for Space Processing of Engineering Materials, Vanderbilt University, Nashville, Tennessee; Space Vacuum Epitaxy Center, University of Houston, Texas; and the Center for Development of Commercial Crystal Growth in Space, Clarkson University, Potsdam, New York.

Specializing in commercial remote sensing applications are the Institute for Technology Development Remote
60 Sensing Center, Stennis Space Center, Mississippi; and the Center for Mapping, Ohio State University, Columbus, Ohio.

Two centers—the Space Power Institute at Auburn University, Auburn, Alabama; and the Center for Space Power, Texas A&M University, College Station, Texas— focus on the commercial development of space power systems. Two others—the Center for Bioservice Space Technologies, University of Colorado, Boulder; and the Center for Cell Research, Pennsylvania State University, University Park, Pennsylvania—are working in the area of
70 bioscience.

The remaining CCDS centers are the Wisconsin Center for Space Automation and Robotics, University of Wisconsin, Madison; the Center for Autonomous and Man-Controlled Robotic and Sensing Systems, Environmental Research Institute of Michigan, Ann Arbor, Michigan; the Center for Materials for Space Structures, Case Western Reserve University, Cleveland, Ohio; and the Center for Advanced Space Propulsion, University of Tennessee Space Institute, Tullahoma, Tennessee.

Reading rate: _____

Questions

1. How many centers for commercial development of space (CCDS) has NASA established? _____

2. Why are the CCDSs important? _____

_____

3. How are these centers funded? _____

_____

4. What is the Center for Macromolecular Crystallography
   at the University of Alabama–Birmingham investigating?

   _____

   _____

5. List four other areas the centers have been investigating.

   _____

   _____

   _____

   _____

6. Describe the breakthrough in superconductivity.

   _____

   _____

7. How much funding does NASA provide for each
   CCDS? _____

   _____

8. Where does the rest of the funding come from?

   _____

9. How long will NASA funding continue? _____

   _____

10. Name two centers that focus on materials research and
    processing: _____

11. Name one center that focuses on commercial remote sensing applications. _____

_____

12. What does the Space Power Institute focus on? _____

_____

Answers

1. 16
2. They are among the most important steps taken to date to encourage greater involvement by the U.S. private sector in space.
3. They are funded by a number of Fortune 500 industrial firms and scores of small businesses.
4. It is investigating the potential of space-grown protein crystals to support new drug research.
5. Possible answers include advanced materials, space remote sensing, space processing, automation and robotics, space propulsion, bioscience, and space power.
6. Dr. Paul Chu and Dr. Mau Wu successfully raised the temperature at which material becomes superconductive.
7. NASA provides annual funding of up to about $1 million for each CCDS.
8. Additional financial and in-kind support comes from industrial affiliates.
9. NASA support for the centers is expected to continue until they can become fully established and self-sufficient.
10. Possible responses: the Center for Advanced Materials, the Consortium for Materials Development in Space, the

Center for Macromolecular Crystallography, the Center for Space Processing of Engineering Materials, the Space Vacuum Epitaxy Center, the Center for Development of Commercial Crystal Growth in Space.

11. Possible responses include the Institute for Technology Development Remote Sensing Center and the Center for Mapping.

12. It focuses on the commercial development of space power systems.

Here are some readings without questions.

Reading 1:
Paper

Paper is a common and abundant material. It can be found anywhere and is so common that it is often taken for granted. Did you ever stop to think where paper comes from and how it is made?

Paper is believed to have been invented by Ts'ai Lu in China. People quickly recognized that Lu was on to something good; as a result, the art of papermaking quickly spread to other continents.

10 How is paper made? The process starts with wood pulp, made by grinding wood. The wood pulp is then washed, bleached, screened, and beaten to achieve the characteristics required for the specific paper—newsprint, fine writing paper, wrapping paper, and so on. The pulp, mixed with water, is poured over a wire screen in one of two machines, the fourdrinier or the cylindric. The former has a belt screen; the latter, a cylindric screen. As water drains through the screen, a layer of fibers forms. The layer is then shaken to turn the fibers in different directions so they form a

20 mat. Then a wet felt belt is pressed against the screen to pick up the paper, which is now ready to be fed through a

series of drying rollers. At the end of the process, the paper is passed through sets of iron rollers that press the paper and smooth its surface. Clay or starch is then added to the paper to help improve printing, texture, and strength. The clay or starch coats the surface, which makes the paper better suited for artwork. All writing papers are "sized," which means that a water-resistant substance is added to the pulp to prevent ink from running when the paper is written on. The
30 paper's last stop is the air dryer. Once it has been dried, it is ready to be shipped.

Each of the above steps must be followed to produce even one sheet of paper. The use of machines cuts down on the time it takes to complete the steps, but none of the stages can be omitted. So the next time you find a few crumpled sheets of paper at the bottom of a drawer, think twice before throwing them out. The time and effort put into their production is worth your consideration.

Reading rate: _____

Reading 2:
Software

The really interesting advances are going to be in software development. Computers haven't made our lives easier. In fact, they have made them more complicated. These things that were supposed to help us deal with information actually have generated much more data to deal with than we ever dreamed possible. Our customers have huge databases that they feel are the assets of the company, but often there are so many data that they are useless. Every single corporation
10 is in this bind. They know they have information about their

clients, their suppliers, their competitors, but there is no way
of getting it together in a way that makes it useful.

Reading rate: _____

Reading 3:
The Days When I Read

Books relieve me from idleness, rescue me from company I
dislike, and blunt the edge of my grief, if it is not too extreme.
They are the comfort and solitude of my old age.

When I am attacked by gloomy thoughts, nothing helps
me so much as running to my books. They quickly absorb
me and banish the clouds from my mind. And they don't
rebel because I use them only for lack of pastimes more
natural and alive. They always receive me with the same
10 welcome.

Yet I make as little use of them, at most, as a miser does
of his gold. Knowing I can enjoy them when I please, I am
satisfied by their mere possession. I never travel without
books, either in war or in peace. Still, I pass days and
months without looking in them. "I'll read by-and-by," I say to
myself, "or tomorrow, or when I choose." Meanwhile, time
slips away, and no harm is done. For you can't imagine how
comforting it is to know they are by my side, to be opened
when I will; and what a refreshment they are to my life.

20 They are the best provisions I have found for this human
journey. And I am sorry indeed for the person of
understanding who is deprived of them.

But reading books is as laborious as any other work, and
can be as great a menace to the health. Neither should we
be deceived by the pleasure of it, which is the same

pleasure that traps the person of affairs, the miser, the libertine, and the ambitious. Books are pleasant enough; but if too much reading impairs the health and spoils our good humor—our most priceless possessions—we should drop it.
30 Nothing we can gain from it will repay us for so great a loss.

In the days when I read a great deal, I used to lay a piece of glass on my page to remove the glare from the paper; and it gave my eyes considerable relief. Even now, at fifty-four years of age, I have no need of spectacles. I can see as far as I ever did, and as well as anyone else. True, if I read in the dusk, I begin to notice that my sight is a little dim and weak. And I always found reading a strain on my eyes, especially at night. They always tired quickly; and I could never stay long at a book, but was forced to have someone
40 read aloud to me.

I like only easy and amusing books that tickle my fancy, or such as give me counsel and comfort. If I use them for study, it is to learn how to know myself, and to teach myself the proper way to live and die.

If someone tells me it degrades the value of the Muses to use them only for sport and pastime, I will answer that such a person little knows the value of pleasure—and it will be all I can do not to add that any other end in life is ridiculous. I live from day to day and, speaking with reverence, only for
50 myself. When young, I studied for show; later, to make myself a little wiser; and now, for pleasure. And never for profit.

I do not bite my nails over the difficulties I encounter in a book. After one or two assaults, I give it up. If I kept at it, I would only lose my time and myself as well; for my mind is good for only one jump. If I can't see a point at the first glance, repeated efforts will do nothing but make it more obscure.

If one book wearies me, I quickly pick up another. I never read except at such hours when the tedium of doing nothing drives me to it.

60   I am not much taken by the new books; the old ones
seem to have more meat and sinew. Nor by the Greeks, for
my judgment can't come into play when my knowledge of a
language is rudimentary and weak.

Reading rate: _____

Reading 4:
The Air We Breathe

People who enjoy exercising outdoors are more vulnerable
to air pollutants such as carbon monoxide and the most toxic
pollutant, ozone, which is at its worst from May through
September. Expanded breathing during exercise means a
higher dose of pollutants enters the lungs, and air is
breathed more deeply. Since most air enters through the
mouth, it undergoes no filtering by the nose.

    If you exercise or engage in strenuous activities outdoors,
10 consider these tips from the American Lung Association to
reduce the chances of any short-term or long-term adverse
health effects.

- Be aware of the quality of the air you breathe. Local air
quality is reported by air pollution control agencies and
the media. Levels of ozone and other pollutants are
reported as a percentage according to federal health
standards, which many experts consider too low. These
standards are the Air Quality Index and Pollutant
Standards Index: 0–50 is good; 50–100 is moderate;
20 100–200 is unhealthful; 200–300 is very unhealthful;
300–500 is hazardous. Atlanta had 6 unhealthful days in
1991; Los Angeles, 109. Washington, D.C., came in with
16 unhealthful days; Houston, 40.
- When an unhealthful ozone level is reported, exercise in
the early morning or evening. The highest ozone levels

typically occur in the afternoon. Exercise indoors when
pollution is high, since the possible damage to health will
far outweigh any benefits from exercise. The elderly,
people with heart or lung disease, and children should
30   remain indoors with the windows closed.

- Avoid exercising near crowded highways. Running in a
typically polluted urban area for 30 minutes is the same
as inhaling the carbon monoxide from 20 cigarettes in
one day.

- Stay at least 30–50 feet away from cars. At traffic lights,
move ahead of the exhaust pipe of the first car, or stay
behind the last car until the light changes.

- If you feel your chest getting tight, or start to cough or
wheeze, stop exercising immediately.

Reading rate: _____

DELL NONFICTION BESTSELLERS